TEACHING SMARTER

TEACHING SMARTER

An
UNCONVENTIONAL
Guide to Boosting
Student Success

Patrick Kelley, M.A.

free spirit
PUBLISHING®

Library of Congress Cataloging-in-Publication Data
Kelley, Patrick Chase.
    Teaching smarter : an unconventional guide to boosting student success / by Patrick Chase Kelley.
        pages cm
    Includes bibliographical references and index.
    ISBN 978-1-57542-492-7 (paperback) — ISBN 1-57542-492-4 (paperback) 1. High school teaching.
2. Effective teaching. 3. Academic achievement. I.Title.
    LB1737.A3K47 2015
    373.1102—dc23

                                                                                    2014040152

Edited by Meg Bratsch and Christine Zuchora-Walske
Cover and interior design by Colleen Rollins

The quotation on page 68 is from Royal Bank of Canada, "The Importance of Teaching," *The Royal Bank Letter* (September–October 1989), www.rbc.com/aboutus/letter/pdf/sep_oct1989.pdf (accessed October 30, 2014).

10 9 8 7 6 5 4 3 2 1
Printed in the United States of America

Free Spirit Publishing Inc.
Minneapolis, MN
(612) 338-2068
help4kids@freespirit.com
www.freespirit.com

To my wife, Dione, who reacted perfectly when I presented the first chapter of this book to her, thus inspiring me to complete the project.

Acknowledgments

Over the last ten years, I have had many exceptional students who have renewed my enjoyment of teaching. Moreover, they have given me the courage to continue attempting new and creative ideas in the classroom. Several students have returned to visit me after completing a four-year university degree, just to tell me that the practical things they learned in my class made a difference. These return visits have meant so much to me. Validations of this type are the reason I teach. Therefore, I send out a sincere thank you to all of my AVID and IB students. They are the best and are a great deal of fun to work with.

My sincere appreciation also goes out to my editor, Meg Bratsch, who from the start has seen the potential of my ideas despite my unusual presentation. I have benefited from her practical and balanced guidance through the editing process. I am also very grateful to Christine Zuchora-Walske, who has helped me make this book more precise and practical than I thought possible. Thank you for challenging me to think down new pathways.

In addition, I would like to thank Chris Peters, perhaps the most passionate AVID coordinator west of the Mississippi. Each year he reminds me of what really motivates the unmotivated student: the student's personal interest and the teacher's concern for the student as a person.

CONTENTS

Digital versions of the handouts on pages 41–42, 102–103, 171, and 174–175, and the Appendix worksheets starting on page 177, can be downloaded at **freespirit.com/teaching-smarter-forms**.

PREFACE

Once upon a time, I served as Advanced Placement coordinator for Cajon High School in San Bernardino. During that time, I received a phone call from one of the admissions officers serving the California State University system. The officer had a series of questions about our grading system for the AP program. I gleaned that we had some students with 4.5 GPAs who had scored miserably on all the AP exams. We also had some students with 2.5 GPAs who had passed all the AP exams. The officer's masked question was obvious: "How is such a thing possible?"

The book you're about to read answers that question. It shows how in many cases, GPAs don't reflect students' knowledge or abilities. Students move through our educational system producing product after product, but this production doesn't necessarily lead to knowledge and skills. Students have done the work, but some of them have learned very little in the process. I hope that by reading this book, you will be encouraged to focus more on imparting knowledge and less on grading products.

We teachers often choose unwisely when it comes to allocating our time and energy. Breaking our entrenched habits may be difficult—it requires a major shift in our thinking. But this effort is worthwhile. None of us got into teaching to do clerical work, but that is what many of us spend a huge amount of time doing, and it often sucks the life out of us. This book shows that teaching doesn't have to be that way. When we stop doing lots of clerical work and free up time for teaching kids more knowledge, more skills, and more strategies for functioning within the flawed and complex U.S. education system, we begin making a real difference. Why? Because now students can focus on learning what we are teaching rather than struggling with logistical obstacles.

Student performance is closely linked to teacher satisfaction and survival. So is the workload heaped upon teachers. In fact, a number of important factors contribute to teacher success. But these issues are seldom—if ever—addressed at American universities. What did *your* college professors fail to teach you about teaching? I'm sure they left out a great deal. They meant well, no doubt. They wanted you to understand all the educational theory behind modern curriculum and teaching practice. But chances are, you left college with many practical questions unanswered. And it's unlikely that the professional development workshops you've attended since then have given you any simple, practical solutions for the day-to-day challenges of a real-life modern classroom. If you're anything like me, you have longed for less theory and more practical advice.

Each chapter of this book offers an answer to a key practical question. Like most books for teachers, it aims to improve both student performance and teacher delivery. But it does so with a much stronger focus on the student viewpoint and the realities of the modern U.S. classroom. It shows teachers how to use student buy-in to build student success. It also shows teachers how to focus on factors within their control in order to avoid burnout.

Any effort to improve student and teacher success must account for the human aspect of teaching and learning. I hope I will convince you that educational success depends on building the strongest relationships possible. I will show you how to build those relationships. Students will work for you if they believe you have their best interests at heart. When that happens, both they and you exit the school year a little bit wiser, a little bit happier, and justifiably proud of your achievements.

Teaching smarter requires a courageous turn toward a less traveled road in modern education. I hope you will enjoy taking a look down that road. And I hope you will soon venture onto it.

INTRODUCTION

As a secondary school educator, I notice that many of my students have the same mindset about education that I proudly sported back in 1986, when I was a student myself. The simple fact is that like me, they judge teachers largely by how easy and realistic it is to get a high grade from them. Although not all students feel this way, the implications for secondary instructors are still huge. In the current educational climate of content standards and high-stakes testing, we are being observed from every angle through a high-powered microscope. Students, families, politicians, and educators can broadcast our perceived flaws and strengths in the twinkling of an eye through social media.

The field of education has produced countless books meant to help teachers. Yet few books deal directly with guiding students toward higher grades and test scores by teaching them practical, time-saving habits that make their work for your class more palatable and profitable. Focusing on grades and test scores has become unpopular in recent years. This unpopularity may be due to flawed education policies that emphasize test scores while neglecting other aspects of education. Or it may be a result of a shift in societal attitudes toward grades; grades simply don't mean what they used to. Whatever the cause of this unpopularity, grades and test scores still affect students' lives and evaluations of teacher performance. So teachers must find a way to help their students boost achievement.

The purpose of this book is to help you use your time and talents more wisely as you guide your students to higher grades and greater engagement. Much of the time we spend working as middle school and high school teachers is wasted in terms of producing higher grades and test scores. We pour a great amount of our energy and talent into jumping through paperwork hoops that leave us feeling burned out and cynical. But you can avoid this fate.

The credentials I offer as an expert in this field are my experiences as a college student both at the graduate and undergraduate levels, my twenty-five years of teaching students at the middle school and high school levels, and most importantly, my efforts at picking the brains and studying the habits of hundreds of students and teachers over the years. For the last twelve years, I have been teaching AVID classes how to get higher grades and SAT scores. AVID stands for Advancement Via Individual Determination. Thousands of middle schools and high schools across the United States offer this educational program. Its purpose is to increase college preparedness and eligibility for all students—especially those in the middle of the academic spectrum. Along the way, my AVID students have shared incredible stories about how they mastered the "game" of education in the most creative ways imaginable. Using these stories, each year I have modified my notes for teaching what amounts to an unconventional course on how to get higher grades. I've accumulated about 150 pages of insights into the educational process for students and teachers. For years, as my students have finally learned how to get through school without making simple grade-destroying mistakes, they've encouraged me to use my teaching notes to write a book so other teachers can offer their students the same help that I offered mine.

In terms of teaching, I've learned something really incredible: much of what we do for hours and hours and hours means very little to some students. Meanwhile, they are passing judgment on us. Their criteria are the simplicity of our grading methods and the perceived fairness of the final grades on their transcripts. If we mess up in grading, very little else matters to them.

We teachers can safely assume that many students are willing to work for higher grades. But the grading process baffles them, and that's why many of them don't do the work—or they do it inefficiently, unsuccessfully, or with great frustration. They are confused at the most elementary level regarding how their final grades are calculated. They struggle to understand how their work is evaluated—often with different standards by different teachers. If we strategize to teach them how the process works, then they will follow it and achieve higher grades.

I have seen this strategy work with my students for more than a decade. I have also seen it work for other teachers, regardless of the subject matter they are teaching. Perhaps the strongest evidence that can be presented to support this strategy is the testimony of countless students. I encourage you to interview students who have mastered higher grades and test scores. I have done so for twenty-five years. I've found that students will readily explain that the key to achieving higher grades is logistical, not intellectual. They will tell you that the devil is in the details of individual teachers' grading methods. We teachers cannot assume that all students have figured out how to get good grades by middle school or high school. They have not! They need our help.

> As teachers, we pour a great amount of our energy and talent into jumping through paperwork hoops that leave us feeling burned out and cynical. But you can avoid this fate.

I wrote this book with the goal of presenting helpful information to you in a way that is not only easy to use, but also enjoyable to read. Please be aware that my writing style is somewhat informal and frank. Be prepared for some humor. My objective in joking and making the occasional outrageous exaggeration is getting you to ponder different perspectives on successful teaching. You should also bear in mind that at times, I break the rules of grammar. Get out your red pen and have at it, if you must. I believe it's about time that we address the subject of education in a more useful and enjoyable way.

This book is designed to be interesting, entertaining, and easy to refer back to. I hope the stories I've told are memorable—they are true unless otherwise stated—and perhaps funny at times. If you remember them and enjoy them, you'll more easily call them to mind and use them in practice.

What you are about to read is a unique guidebook. It should answer any question you have about helping your students get higher grades with several examples that you can pick from. Most of these suggestions simply are not discussed anywhere in the field of education—but I believe they should be. Whether you agree or disagree, I think you'll find this book is worth the read. If you apply the information you learn here, you will save yourself a ton of work—and that is key to surviving and thriving as an educator.

About This Book

This book has two main parts:

Part 1 offers simple and practical suggestions on how to tackle the teacher workload in a fraction of the time you might currently be spending, while helping your students achieve greater success in test scores and grades. Each chapter in Parts 1 and 2 contains an Action Plan offering specific strategies that are simple and easy to use.

> *This book is a reminder that you can choose a different journey. This journey departs from the heavily traveled highway of paperwork to the less traveled road of positive interaction and relationships—or, we could say, from the clerical profession to the teaching profession.*

Part 2 shows you how to teach students the path to higher grades and improved test scores by helping them understand the logistics of academics.

At the end of this book you will find ten reproducible handouts that you can use directly in the classroom. These worksheets come with built-in instructions and are easy to use. Please also visit Free Spirit's website to download these handouts in digital form. See page ix for the website link to digital versions of the forms.

How to Use This Book

I recommend that when you first dig into this book, you read it in the sequence in which it's written. This approach will introduce you to key ideas, examples, and strategies early on. This information will help you make the best possible use of the concepts and advice that come later in the book. After you're familiar with the whole book, you can dip into it here and there as needed.

It would be helpful to put this book on your desk, next to your lesson plan book. That way you will have a quick reference to the types of activities that often benefit students. The book will remind you to save yourself the work of grading much of the mindless copying that some students produce. It will also be an excellent step-by-step guide to lessons and lectures you can add to your subject matter. The handouts are complete lessons in themselves. If you have this book on your desk, then at times you can simply read a chapter out loud to your class. For example, you might read aloud Chapter 15: Teach Your Students How to Be Organized or any of Chapters 19 through 26, on the eight grade destroyers. It will take less than five minutes and could be a good warm-up activity.

Please take the time early in the year to have a Socratic Seminar–type discussion with your students using the guidance provided in Chapter 5 of this book. It will endear your students to you and you to them. Students of all ability levels will listen and learn more from your teaching strategies, because they will believe that you care about their goal of getting higher grades. They will see that your passion is not just for the subject matter but also for their personal success.

Remember, much of the work that we teachers create with our lesson plans bears no fruit in our students but the sour fruit of product without knowledge. This book is a reminder that you can choose a different journey. This journey departs from the heavily traveled highway of paperwork to the less traveled road of positive interaction and relationships—or, we could say, from the clerical profession to the teaching profession.

Highlight and share relevant sections of the book with students who are seeking higher grades but have yet to figure out the methods. You can debate and discuss the ideas in class with students, especially during advisory time, or with faculty members during department or faculty meetings. It won't be boring. Who wouldn't be interested in higher grades with less paperwork?

Imagine that you are planning to give a test, and you know that your students will not study for it until the night before. At the start of the week, why not go over Chapters 15 and 26 so that they will not procrastinate?

Picture yourself dealing with a bright student who fails to turn in every third assignment for whatever reason. He receives several zeros in the course of a semester, changing his grade from an A to a D. We have an obligation as educators to address such matters. Use the lessons in this book to do so without causing personal offense. If the student won't listen to you, his parent most likely will.

Let's say you have several students who will not take the standardized test seriously. They simply feel that the test is too long, too boring, too unfair, too whatever. What can you do? Chapters 5 and 27 will make a difference in both their attitudes toward the test and their attitudes toward academics.

Lastly, you can use this book to help students overcome the hidden pitfalls of grading. Show them how any test or teacher grading system has specific expectations, glitches, nuances, and inconsistencies that students can master to achieve higher scores. Often it is the grading system or test structure—not the subject matter—that defeats students academically. When a student is defeated by the system and not the subject matter, you can fix the problem in a logical way by helping the student learn the system. Share this book with students, their parents, and other educators as you do so.

Every year a huge number of educators leave the teaching profession because of the ever-increasing workloads and responsibilities placed upon them. They lose their joy in teaching. In fact, in most states, the exodus numbers are staggering. Between 40 and 50 percent of new teachers leave within the first five years of teaching. And what about the survivors? Are they despairing, too? Yes, some of them are. Those teachers need more than the usual pep talk about how they are shaping the future and making a difference in lives of children. Teachers already believe that. They need practical plans for shaping the future in a way that will not sap the life out of them. The same is true for students and parents. They don't need to hear "work harder," but rather "here is how you do it."

Here is how you do it. This book will show you the way. Take the road less traveled and enjoy the journey to *Teaching Smarter*.

I'd love to receive any feedback that you care to share with me. If you have feedback to offer or questions that are not addressed in this book, write to me in care of Free Spirit Publishing, 217 Fifth Avenue North, Suite 200, Minneapolis, MN 55401-1299. You can also contact me by visiting my website at www.patrickkelleybooks.com.

Patrick Kelley

PART 1
Decrease Your Workload and Increase the Payoff

I suggest that you review key portions of this part of the book before planning major assignments and exams. This strategy will save you a great deal of work. I have written this section with that purpose in mind. The practical suggestions you will find here are easy to implement.

CHAPTER 1

What Assignments Are Worth Giving?

You might have any number of valid reasons for giving an assignment. But which assignments are actually worth giving? Let's define a worthwhile assignment in the following three ways:

1. There is a high probability that the student will do the actual work and not plagiarize or copy.

2. There is a high probability that the student will remember the work beyond the test.

3. The student can redo the work if needed, so that eventually your learning objectives are met.

Point 1: Give Work That Students Will Do, Not Copy

Remember, many students are:

- Masters at cutting and pasting

- Masters at the email typeface change (They share the assignment by email, but before printing it, they change the typeface so that it looks slightly different to the teacher.)

- Masters of the slight paraphrase

- Masters at cheating in ways that we cannot even imagine

- Masters at doing their homework while texting, watching videos, and listening to music

- Masters at producing a product to receive a grade but learning nothing or very little in the process

Remember this maxim when you're giving an assignment: "If it can be copied, it will be copied." If students can produce—or perhaps we should say reproduce—an assignment with the help of someone or something, many of them will. The digital age has magnified an old problem. Today's students are going online to find answers, which are easy to copy and paste. It's also easy to reproduce another student's work digitally. We must deal logically with the temptation modern students face. There is no point in ignoring the reality of such dishonesty and no way to defeat it. Therefore, we should adjust to the reality and react wisely.

Perhaps the dreaded worksheet is the best example of an assignment that's likely to be copied. Here is the typical worksheet assignment: it asks the student to find the answers to selected important questions by reviewing relevant material. Sounds great, right? Wrong! Many kids will simply Google the questions or copy answers from one or two students who did all the work. When this happens—and it is common—all you have your taught students is that your assignments are easy to cheat on. Don't fool yourself into thinking your students are worried that if they don't do the work now, they'll suffer on the test later. They're not thinking that way; that part of their brain is still developing.

Many students will study for the test when and if the test comes. And of course, they'll wait until the night before, because they think there's no use storing all that stuff too long in their brain; they might forget it.

Another aspect of this problem is making homework assignments worth too many points. For example, some teachers make homework worth 25 percent or more of the final grade. This habit of overvaluing homework just contributes to grade inflation.

Here's the bottom line: due to the potential for dishonesty, offering assignments on which cheating is easy or expedient is not helpful to learning or motivation. Assignments of this type pose another major danger to education and learning: education in general becomes a mundane hoop-jumping exercise. Furthermore, spending hours grading mass-produced paperwork takes a great deal of time that you could better spend preparing lessons. Finally, easily copied assignments such as worksheets reinforce poor study habits—habits of work without thought. Cranking out a product without gaining knowledge in the process is too often accepted as worthy of a grade or reward.

Instead, give assignments that are not easily copied, such as essays and opinion-oriented work. Require higher-level thinking; use prompts such as *judge*, *evaluate*, *assess*, and *predict*. For example, cartoon analysis and document-based questions (DBQs) are often the basis for Advanced Placement (AP) and Common Core social studies essays, in which the essay prompt contains relevant primary source material.

Point 2: Give Work That Students Will Remember

A valid assignment should have strong potential for teaching knowledge or skills that will last beyond the next test or assessment. How do we make assignments memorable? There is no easy recipe. But if students know that the work they do in class or as homework will show up again on a test in almost the same format, then they will pay closer attention. Let's rephrase this. Put your homework questions on the test. Put your classroom activity worksheet questions on the test.

But why would you do this? Doesn't this make the test too easy?

We want learning to be easy, don't we? We are not trying to trick students, but teach them. When you put your homework and classwork on the test in similar language, this helps students connect the work with the test, and that connection creates buy-in. Buy-in creates positive attitudes about your teaching methods, and that goes a long way toward getting students to do work that they will remember past the test.

When students encounter their classwork and homework on a test, they'll become believers. As they move on to new assignments, they will tell themselves to pay attention, thinking, "Okay, I will need this later, because it will be on the test."

If you want students to remember what you have taught *past* the test, then tell them that this information will appear throughout the entire year on future tests. I approach this by having a section in every test with the heading "Questions from Past Tests." In addition, I remind my students that they are accountable *all year* for any test item. And I let them keep copies of all tests to study from.

You might say, "Oh, no—now you have gone too far! They will just study for the test by memorizing all the questions and answers." Some may try; after all, they are kids. If you're worried about this, change the wording of the questions slightly, but keep the concepts the same.

In the end, you will challenge your students to learn beyond the next test. You will make them think about remembering facts and skills throughout the entire year. Students will know that whatever you teach is not going away after you test them on it.

Let me ask you a question to conclude this section. In terms of factual knowledge (not higher-level thinking), how many facts would you like your students to know—in history, math, biology, English, you name it? How about two hundred? Four hundred? Five hundred? Well, if you give your students two hundred questions once, if they are smart, they may remember twenty in the course of a year. But if you repeat those two hundred questions scattered throughout all your tests, you get improved retention. The saying "repetition is the mother of retention" is true. For example, when I started using this method, my students' standardized tests scores improved from 50 percent proficient to 70 percent. Results will vary, of course. Children and teenagers who are recovering from boring class syndrome or overtesting may respond differently and require further educational assistance.

Point 3: Give Work That Students Can Redo

A worthwhile assignment is one on which all students can get an A or B if they redo it enough times. This idea may sound strange at first, I know. But hear me out.

When you give a homework or classwork assignment, view it as a football coach views the Thursday practice before the big Friday game. The Thursday practice does not count in the official football standings, but it may determine whether the team wins or loses on Friday.

You see, classwork and homework are just that: practice. They are not the big game; they are not the test. They should not count in the standings. Yet we all grade homework and classwork, don't we? Why? Because we believe that if we don't assign points, then no one will do the work? I urge you to move away from this idea as much as you can.

Practice is for fixing bad habits and reinforcing good habits. It should play a limited role in determining the final score of the game. Classwork and homework are about effort. If a student is getting the work wrong (D or F quality), give it back and have the student do it again until it is right (A or B quality). Then and only then should you record the grade.

Who cares that the good grade was not earned on the first try? Remember, homework and classwork are practice. A football coach wouldn't stop drilling a play after one botched attempt, and neither should you. By giving students a second chance, you are teaching them not to quit. You are teaching them that they can meet the standard. You are building knowledge, resilience, and self-esteem.

Students will love and respect this approach. They will know you are not handing them an unearned grade or watering anything down. Rather, you are showing them that you will accept only work that meets the standard. And when they get that A or B, they feel good.

Now, if you are worried that this approach will cause grade inflation, then the solution is quite simple: make classwork and homework only 10 percent of the final grade. This strategy will produce fair results. If students earn good grades on their homework and classwork—regardless of how many attempts they must make or how the work is weighted—they will have learned what they need in order to get good grades on tests. On the flip side, if you accept sub-par classwork or homework, you can expect similar work on the test. Learning does not happen by osmosis.

> Homework and classwork are practice. A football coach wouldn't stop drilling a play after one botched attempt, and neither should you. By giving students a second chance, you are teaching them not to quit. You are teaching them that they can meet the standard. You are building knowledge, resilience, and self-esteem.

Please don't think that you can't let students redo classwork and homework because it will mean extra work for you. You'll actually save time and effort if you get students into good habits from the beginning. When we don't teach proper work habits from the start, we end up doing extra work in the form of constant remediation. The longer we wait, the more ingrained students' problems become.

ACTION PLAN

Assign work that is worth giving:

- Assignments in which the information and work done will appear in the next test and in future tests in a similar form

- Assignments that are not easily copied, such as essays and opinion-oriented work

- Assignments that allow for a redo

- Quick write-ups of what was learned

- Open-ended questions

- Think-Pair-Share discussions

- Socratic Seminar reviews

- Flash card practice in pairs (See page 111 for details.)

- Essays that mimic the objectives and standards word for word or nearly so

- Selected readings with sworn statements (A sworn statement is something like: "I, Jane Doe, swear on my Aunt Sally's Holy Bible that I actually read this material—every last word of it!" [See page 106.])

Avoid assigning work that has little value for standards and state testing:

- Word searches

- Reports

- Art projects (Sorry, often they don't help on many levels—at least not in core content areas. They might be worthwhile for motivation, though.)

- Mindless vocabulary copying

- Crosswords (These are typically copied from the first student who finds the answers.)

- Posters with pictures, captions, and whatnot (They look nice, but they usually take you nowhere.)

- Section reviews (unless you put these questions on the test)

- Worksheets of any kind (unless you put the information on the test)

- Reading assignments without direction (Try the sworn statement to encourage completion.)

- Group work in which one person does most of the submitted work

CHAPTER 2

How to Grade Forty Essays in Forty Minutes—Accurately

When it comes to grading student work, I have found after twenty-five years of teaching that with few exceptions, the only assignments that need my personal attention are essays. Your teaching assistant (TA) or student helpers can grade just about everything else in your assignment arsenal. If you are good at teaching how to write an analytical essay, in no time at all your students will be just as accurate as you are at grading an essay. But students will still want you to read their essays—and so you should—but don't obligate yourself to read anything else. Your time is better spent creating effective lessons than grading paperwork.

Does this chapter title really suggest that you can grade forty four-page essays full of sloppy handwriting, terrible grammar, and poorly expressed thoughts and ideas in less than one hour? Yes—and, I might add, you can do it with precision. Don't worry; I am not trying to sell you a bridge in Brooklyn. Until 2007, I would never have believed forty essays in one hour was possible either. Here is how I changed my mind.

Grade 800 Essays in Eight Hours? On What Planet?

I was on a plane traveling to Louisville, Kentucky, to grade AP U.S. history essays for the College Board. It was my first time. I was told that the experience would really revolutionize my teaching of the AP course and would be memorable. It was!

On the plane I overheard a group of teachers discussing the grading process. I thought that I must have misheard the numbers. One gentleman was bragging that he could grade 400 essays a day. Actually, he said 800, but I just cannot accept that, so I will quote him as saying 400, which I now believe is possible. But I didn't believe it back then. Remember, these AP essays average about four pages each, and graders must follow a very specific rubric. Essay grading is checked and double-checked and matched with computer calculations on the multiple-choice test to make sure the essay correlates to the multiple-choice portion. The College Board is serious. It wants accuracy, and it doesn't play games.

I consider myself lazy. I'm someone who's always looking for the easy way out. I'm also a fast reader. So I figured if anyone could read 800 essays in eight hours, it was me. On day seven of this eight-day joyfest, I graded 200 essays without complaint from the powers that be. The computer said the multiple-choice scores matched my essay scoring.

The table head agreed with my scores when she randomly checked several of my graded essays. I worried that I might be off, because I was a rookie and a complainer about the poor quality of work the nation's best and brightest were producing. But evidently, after a few days I had gotten the hang of it by sheer repetition and determination.

> You don't need to do a point-by-point count as you read an essay. In the end, simply ask yourself, "To what extent did the student answer the prompt with examples?"

As with most skills, practice is really valuable in grading essays. We teachers can become accurate and fast essay graders if we just stick with it. (And so can our students!) Essays are so much work at first that we often quit too soon or avoid giving essay assignments altogether—and that is a mistake.

For three years after my experience in Louisville, I pondered the possibility of reading 800 essays in eight hours. I could not get it out of my head. How did that guy do it? If I could just grade half as fast, I wouldn't mind giving essays to my students more often. And that would really make a difference in my teaching.

I still don't know exactly how that fellow did 800 in eight hours, but I can now complete 400 accurately in that time. One essay per minute is not an outrageous goal. I am living proof that you don't have to be gifted with special memory abilities to grade forty essays in forty minutes. I have even taught my students how to do it.

If you keep assigning essays to your students despite the horrific amount of grading work that essays entail, your determination to get through them will enhance your speed and accuracy. I find that my eyes and thoughts are so focused when grading an essay—just from lots of practice—that I can read and apply my rubric of choice in about one minute per four-page essay. And I rarely get any complaints about my accuracy.

Obviously you cannot mark the essay as you read it—there's no time for grammar corrections or comments. And students really don't care about that stuff anyway; they just look for the grade, because I offer one-on-one conferences if they don't agree with their scores. If the conferencing proves my accuracy to them, as it usually does, few students challenge my essay grades ever again. I love the challenge of such conferences, even if I am wrong and have to change a grade, because they give me a chance to show kids that I care, that I am approachable, and that I'm on their side. Humility in a teacher is more powerful than pride. I want my kids to see that in me, and if they don't, I know what to work on.

You see, a good essay, just like a good book, has a feel to it. Sometimes you can be deceived, but generally you know quite soon where things are going. Does this mean that you don't actually have to read every word on every page? No, not at all. I am just saying that you can move quite fast after practice. You can quickly see the writer's thought process, and experience tells you what the score is according to the rubric.

You don't need to do a point-by-point count as you read an essay. In the end, simply ask yourself, "To what extent did the student answer the prompt with examples?" The beauty of this simple question is that it clears your mind to focus sharply on the goal. When you are judging an essay, a lot can cloud your brain. You need simplicity of thought and clarity of purpose. If you do not allow your mind to be distracted with nonessential details, you will almost always be spot-on. Why? Because as you practice, you'll develop an intuition that allows you to move faster and faster through these essays. I know this may be hard to accept, but I challenge you to prove me wrong. With any skill that we may wish to develop, some of us are naturally more gifted and some are less so, but practice increases speed and accuracy for everyone.

Perhaps you are hoping for a secret little method to help you learn how to speed through those dreaded essays. Try this. Grade the essays in the manner described above, challenging yourself to complete the essay in two minutes per essay—no matter what. Just give each essay the grade that intuition tells you the essay deserves. After grading, give the stack of essays to your TA or your brightest student and have your helper do a random quality check of your scoring, by considering elements from the rubric. Discuss the results, notice your tendencies, and make adjustments as needed. Over time, drop your time limit down to one minute per essay.

TA or Student Helper Comments and Peer Editing

I said was lazy, and I wasn't kidding. Getting fast and good at essay grading means less work. After I increased my speed and skill, I decided to continue down my lazy path of avoiding needless work. I figured out how to delegate it.

Be aware that much of what you are looking for in an essay can be highlighted for you before you begin reading. This is a great time saver. It can bring you closer to making forty in forty a reality. It is the rubric that slows the scoring process. So ask yourself, "How much legwork can I get done by having others mark essays ahead of time for specific rubric points so I don't have to stop for the rubric point by point?" Let's say the rubric has you looking for ten items, and eight of the ten are quite tangible and plain to anyone. If you have your teaching assistant (TA) or a student helper find those eight items and score them for you, you can focus on the remaining two. Using this strategy, you can slash your grading time by 75 percent or more.

> The value of peer editing cannot be overstated. It is an unmatched time saver, a powerful teaching tool, and a strong confidence builder.

Here is another great tip: Have your TA or a student helper score the spelling and grammar and make comments on the essays before you read the essays. These comments can be about the thesis, the organization, the historical evidence, the analytical thinking, the implications, and so on. If the TA or student helper makes accurate comments, you can grade even more quickly.

It is reassuring to students to know that more than one person looked at their work. That brings us to peer editing—the most effective way to save time and score forty in forty. Peer editing is having students grade one another's essays before or after your reading.

Here's an example. Let's say my students have spent the last forty minutes writing an AP or International Baccalaureate (IB)–style analytical essay in class. They are all addressing the same prompt. Ten minutes of class time remain. I say to the entire class, "Switch papers and follow my instructions to the letter. Do what I say at the exact moment I tell you. Get your act together mentally right now and focus." I say this in such a kind manner that they just love me. (Really, it is all in the tone.)

> *Having students score essays using a rubric makes them better writers because they become more aware of what they must do to earn high scores.*

Then I say, "Step one. Read the first two paragraphs, find the thesis, and underline it." I pause for a couple of minutes while the students read. "Rate the thesis on a scale of one to ten in terms of how well it addresses the prompt. Put your score in the margin with a comment if you like."

Next I say, "Now read the next page and put a check mark next to each fact that supports the student's thesis." I pause for a couple of minutes while the kids do this. "Count up and write the number of check marks, so that the student knows exactly how much evidence the essay presented. Note whether the evidence was listed or analyzed. Listing is not as good, as you already know."

I ask the students at this point to make some comments in the margins regarding how well this essay answers the question and follows the rubric's expectations, both stated and implied. I could go on and on with more details, but surely you are getting the point and can implement this type of peer editing strategy. In this book, I want to get you thinking about what *you* can do in *your* classroom. There's no need to quibble with the minor details of my own methods. Just keep this in mind: the less you play the role of clerk and the more time you spend planning lessons and teaching students, the greater success you will enjoy.

The value of peer editing cannot be overstated. It is an unmatched time saver, a powerful teaching tool, and a strong confidence builder. Peer editing validates a student's need to know that someone actually read and examined his or her work in a thoughtful way. The more people that read the work, the more credible the grade, and the higher the student's accountability. Moreover, students do not want to be embarrassed by having their peers read weak work, so next time they are motivated to prepare more. Students really will comment on how much this helps them.

Finally, peer editing broadens a student's perspective. It is hard to write well if you have only seen your own writing. When students see how others attack a problem, this gives them ideas. And if students write better than what they are reading while peer editing, this gives them confidence. Having students score essays using a rubric makes them better writers because they become more aware of what they must do to earn high scores. Not enough practice is the biggest reason for low test scores.

ACTION PLAN

1. Make the scoring rubric simple. Break it down to the essentials. Keep the principles in your head.

2. Now challenge yourself to score each essay in two minutes or less, no matter what. Adjust your reading speed to make that happen. This is possible even if you are a slow reader. It just takes a little practice. You will soon find that you can score as accurately in two minutes as you can in twenty. Before you criticize this claim, try it.

3. Employ TAs or student helpers or use peer editing as described in this chapter. You will find that you can save a great deal of time having students apply the rubric and mark the essay so you only need to confirm the grade after you read the essay.

4. Remember that peer editing is not only a time saver but also a great teaching tool and a way to validate students' hard work.

5. Offer a one-on-one conference for a dissatisfied student only after two or three other students have also read the student's essay. Few complainers will take you up on this, but if they do, conferences offer a great opportunity to build rapport and cement your reputation as an accurate grader.

6. Remember that accurately grading forty four-page essays in forty minutes does not happen without practice, but it will happen—and it will revolutionize your teaching.

CHAPTER 3

How to Make the Best Use of Your TA (And What to Do If You Don't Have One)

Most secondary schools offer some support to teachers in the form of teaching assistants (TAs). How can you make the best use of your TA? It's quite simple: have your TA do everything except the final scoring on essays. If there is anything clerical a TA shouldn't do for you . . . well . . . it does not readily come to mind. If you really think about it, you will find that you can avoid much of the paperwork you're currently doing because it is self-created. And in reality, anyone can do it. Have your TA do all the mindless work that engulfs and strangles you. Take the clerical work out of your job. Give the time and energy you save back to the kids in the form of creative lessons and personal attention.

Here's a mantra to remember in your daily work: "If it is not absolutely, 100 percent necessary for me to do this paperwork myself, I will not do it." Let it go. No one has ever learned more because you did paperwork from administration or from the district or from your own organizational method.

Questions You May Have

Before I continue, let me address four key questions that my assertions may have raised.

What Kinds of Clerical Work Can TAs Do?

A successful teacher is a good delegator of redundant tasks. For example, your TA can collect and pass back work. Your TA can alphabetize student assignments for easy recording. Your TA can organize books, workbooks, and materials. Your TA can update progress charts and list missing assignments.

Your TA can also lighten your load of administrative work. Most schools or districts require constant posting of standards, objectives, and daily agendas. This posting is time-consuming and energy-draining. If you teach multiple subjects, you may be at the board several times a day changing your postings. To save this time for more constructive work, you could train your TA to check your lesson plan book daily and do this clerical work for you.

Here's a mantra to remember in your daily work: "If it is not absolutely, 100 percent necessary for me to do this paperwork myself, I will not do it."

TAs can also help you with all the surveys you must record, parental letters you must gather and distribute, and student statistics you must document. Some of these tasks may require your personal attention by law. But chances are, most of them don't. I have saved hundreds of hours annually asking myself two simple questions: "What part of this task must I, by law, complete?" and "What legwork or setup for this task can my TA do?" The answers to these questions may surprise you and free up lots of your time.

What If I Don't Have a TA?

If you do not have a TA (student or adult), train all your current students to do your paperwork on a rotating schedule. Perhaps they can count this work as community service hours. Doing some work for you and their peers builds appreciation both ways. It also helps students understand the logistics of teaching, learning, and responsibility in the real world.

Don't worry about critics who say that delegating your paperwork is exploitation. Some people might say that it is not a student's job to help you. On the face of it, that seems true. A student's job is to learn. However, this statement does not account for the fact that when students help you correct the work you've assigned, they are learning and relearning the topic with each paper they grade.

In reality, after doing this work for you, students are much more knowledgeable than they were beforehand. In fact, I have often heard my TAs and helpers teaching other students the work that they've just graded for me. When someone asks them, "How did you learn all this stuff?" they respond, "I just read about it when I was helping Mr. Kelley."

Moreover, there is a great sense of ownership and team building that occurs when students work hand in hand with a teacher—even when the task is clerical in nature. Most schools have mission statements asserting that students will become "responsible citizens" and "team players" and will "contribute to the community." Working as a TA provides students with job training for the real world. It teaches responsibility and builds respect.

Is It Ethical to Let Students Judge Other Students' Work?

The final judgment of any student work rests with you, the teacher—not with the TA or student helper. When you allow students to take turns in the role of TA, they will be reviewing and analyzing other students' work, not passing judgment on it.

Most students learn best with concrete examples, so they benefit greatly when they see multiple examples of finished assignments. Can you imagine being asked to build a house without ever seeing one—and then never getting the chance to fully compare your house to other houses? We ask students to do that every day. We tell them what we want. We model what we think they need. We illustrate it, and then they try to do what we ask. But students rarely see multiple examples of finished products. I think students need to see several finished products in order to cement learning. They need to be able to compare and contrast before they start a task, to avoid mistakes and select strategies. After the task is done, they need to see what their peers did in order to validate learning and generate future creativity. When you employ students in the grading process, you are giving them finished products both before the task and after the task. This makes learning meaningful and memorable.

What About Privacy and Fairness?

Perhaps you are worried about the appearance of unfairness or invasion of privacy that might come with using students on a rotating TA schedule. This is a valid concern. You can head off such worries by being proactive. Take the time to explain fully—both in class to your students and in your syllabus for parents and administrators—that *all* students will be working together to offer *feedback* on assignments, before final products are submitted *for your assessment*. If students, parents, and administrators all understand from the outset how things will work in your classroom, then they will not get the idea that students are running the show. I have found that when I present my methods in this way, I get nothing but praise from everyone.

Making a Difference

I had an epiphany about paperwork a few years ago. You see, at the school where I teach, the graduates get special pins with their caps and gowns. They are supposed to give the pins to people who have made a difference in their lives. It is quite an honor to get one. On graduation day, teachers wear these pins on their gowns and show them off to the world.

I always had a fair number of pins to wear, and I felt proud of them. Then one year, I spent a great deal of time on clerical work and other so-called obligations. Oh, I was "good" that year; the pedagogy and competency were oozing out of my pores. How many pins did I get that year? Two. I couldn't believe it! It was my best year of teaching—or so I thought. Yet I got two pins, and Mr. Peters had twelve! He was good, too, but what the heck had happened to me?

Peters and I talked before playing tennis one day. The problem soon became apparent. I'd lost track of the whole point of teaching: to make a difference in students' lives. If I wanted to make a difference, then I needed to spend my time getting to know the kids and helping them personally—not just doing paperwork, writing lesson plans, doing research, and crafting presentations. I needed to care about and talk and laugh and empathize with my students a lot. To make that possible, I needed to let other things go.

The next year, my gown looked like I'd just robbed a jewelry store. One of my colleagues said, "Dude, you're the Pinster! The Pinmaster! The Pinnogram! The Pinnonator!" I was embarrassed, actually. I'd left the previous year's pins on my gown—so I did cheat a little. But this experience taught me an important lesson. Getting more than a dozen pins comes only from building relationships with students. Kids did not give me pins because I taught them to write like Mary Shelley or to think like Socrates. They gave me pins because I listened to them and made them laugh. I was able to do that largely because I let go of paperwork.

Train Your TAs or Student Helpers

Train your TAs or student helpers by working with them at first. With your helper at your side, select four samples from the stack of student work to be graded. One sample is of high quality, one is of medium quality, and one is of low quality. The last sample is a random selection used to test your helper's competence. Now mark the paper while talking your helper through your objectives and expectations:

Teacher: "Hey, do you see this right here? This is analysis. This is good. Do you know why?"

Helper: "Yeah, I see it. He actually answered the question directly."

Teacher: "Right—exactly. So what would you give this paper?"

Helper: "Nine points out of ten."

Teacher: "I agree. What about this one?"

Helper: "It is not quite as good. She is trying to answer the question, but I am not completely following her answer."

Teacher: "I agree, but this is average for the standard and typical for this class. What grade do we give for an average or typical response?"

Helper: "Seven out of ten, I suppose."

Teacher: "Look at this last one."

Helper: "This is a piece of crap."

Teacher: "That might be your gut reaction, but never write that on the paper. It is not encouraging to the student. What could you say that would help preserve his ego and motivate him to do better?"

Helper: "How about 'Redo this paragraph right here and turn this back in for a grade. If you have any questions, see the teacher.'"

Teacher: "Good. I like that because it makes this assignment a learning tool. You are improving his skills without destroying his motivation. Now I am going to select a random paper from the stack. I want you to write the score you would give this student on a separate piece of paper. Don't show me the score until I do the same, and we will see if our scores match."

This is good training not only for TAs and student helpers, but for all students. Use this activity to train your entire class if you prefer grading work in class by having students exchange papers. After some training and practice, the quality of your students' work will improve noticeably. Moreover, when students see how other students accomplish a task, they will cement their own learning.

Remember, you are a teacher. Teachers should, above all, *teach*. Teaching is too important to play second fiddle to clerical work. Many educators express frustration that a lot of their job requirements have nothing at all to do with helping young people; they're just shuffling papers. Paperwork has rarely—if ever—solved any problems in education. If you want more time with students, you have to simplify. Meditate on what really has to be done. Meditate on what really matters. Meditate on what really will cause change. Meditate on letting go of the paperwork.

ACTION PLAN

1. Ask yourself, "Can someone other than me do this paperwork?" The answer is yes. Have the courage to let this happen.

2. Take the time to train your students so they can help you grade papers. Remember, they are learning a great deal as they help you.

3. Take the time to use peer editing (see Chapter 2). It is a masterful teaching tool and time saver.

4. Prioritize your day to be heavy on personal time spent with individual students.

CHAPTER 4

The Teacher Likability Factor

I started teaching in 1986 for the Los Angeles Unified School District (LAUSD), the second largest district in the nation. I was assigned to Mount Vernon Junior High School. I was hired as a math teacher. I had taken two or three math classes in college, and that was enough back then to get an Emergency Teaching Credential in math.

On my first day of class, however, I was assigned as a sub for the physical education department. About fifty students were on the roster, and we met in the auditorium for roll call. I don't remember why we didn't just go outside, since the school was overcrowded, but there we were. I had received two weeks of LAUSD training on how to be a math teacher. This boot camp was quite well done, but nothing could have prepared a small-town Vermonter for what was about to happen to me as a substitute PE teacher in a big-city school.

You see, the English or theater department also used the auditorium, and those students had been practicing for a play. On the stage they'd left wigs, ropes, medieval costumes, fake swords and rocks, and other stuff that looked really, really, really cool to a teenager. (It looked cool to me, too, I must admit.) As fast as a pit bull on a pot roast, my students donned the costumes and were swinging across the stage on the ropes. We even had music. I don't know where it came from, but it was perfect for the occasion. The students broke out dancing.

Now let me pause here for a moment. What would you have done as this scene began to unfold? Well, I am sure it would have been more dignified than what I did. Vermonters rarely dance, unless perhaps an insect is in the wrong location. I personally could only tolerate dancing to impress a girl—or now, my wife. In the past, to attempt dancing in public, I'd almost always needed a favorite beverage near at hand for encouragement. However, on this day I attempted to dance without them. I did not know what else to do; nothing in my training dealt with this situation. For the first time in my life, I thought that if I just put forth a little effort, I might be a great dancer. I might even be the best dancer out there, because it would be a stretch to call what the students were doing dancing.

All my life I had been told—and had come to believe—that I could not dance. But judging by the response from these kids, I was in fact the best dancer that they had ever seen. They had never seen moves like mine—especially to the kind of music they were playing.

First there was a deafening silence as all the students stopped to watch me, wide-eyed with amazement. Then they burst into laughter. The eruption of mirth took a good two minutes to subside. When it did end, I said absolutely nothing. My dancing had said it all. I just called the roll while the students stood in perfect silence and awe. We walked out to the basketball courts. I organized several games. Before the day was over, almost every student in the school of 2,400 knew my name was "Kelley—He Got Moves." That label stayed with me for an entire semester.

Completely by accident, I had learned what is arguably the most important lesson in teaching. That is: if you want to reach the students, you must make them laugh and let them see something likable in you. Let them see something real, something vulnerable, something human. Let them see someone willing to take a chance and make a mistake in public. Perhaps you have noticed that one of the greatest fears of teenagers is the fear of embarrassing themselves in public. In part, they fear being judged adversely. When you show them that you are open to judgment, you also show them there is nothing to be afraid of. This will make learning feel safe, and they so desperately need that.

I firmly believe that learning cannot happen without a relationship between teacher and student. And no one wants to know you if you are not at least somewhat likable. I call this the likability factor. Likability will serve you more than any education degree.

Likability: In Depth

Let's define likability in greater detail. You don't have to be a great dancer, comedian, storyteller, or anything like that to win over kids. The likability factor's key ingredient is honesty—pure and honest responses without malice or agendas or judgments.

If you want to win the hearts of students, tell them the truth when they ask you a question. They don't often get that at home or from adults in general. Please don't misunderstand me here. I am not suggesting you should ever be honest to the point of rudeness or that you should get too personal about yourself or your students. You must always respect the boundary between student and teacher. It is a big mistake to cross it or even flirt with doing so.

For example, if you are too busy to talk with a student or you are not mentally prepared for the drama the student is displaying, you don't want to say "I can't deal with you right now!" Instead, say something like this in your own way: "Hey, Maria, the question you have deserves more attention than just a quick answer, and that's all I have time for right now. Perhaps you have a valid point on how I graded your work differently from Angela's. I want to hear what you have to say. Can you come by at lunch or during the first five minutes after school with that assignment in your hand?"

No matter what you say, kids will challenge all your personal qualities—your consistency, your honesty, your integrity, your fairness, your attitude, and your patience, just to name a few. But here is the point of this chapter: your response to them should always be a model of self-control, humility, and honesty. To be specific, you should never give the impression—let me repeat, the *impression*—that you are taking things personally.

Consider reacting this way: A student comes in to talk with you about his graded paper. You are confident you graded the paper accurately, but the student is dissatisfied. The thing to do is praise him for caring about his grade. Praise him for having the courage to speak with you—and for whatever else you can think of. Make him feel good. Why? Well, besides the fact that this is the right thing to do, let's look at the situation selfishly.

Your reputation is everything in this career. If students start talking about you as if you are a hothead or an uncaring ape or whatever, then you've got a whole new set of problems, and life is going to be stressful. You have probably heard with your own ears and seen with your own eyes that if students don't like you, they won't listen when you talk or turn in assignments when you give them. They are not mature enough to know that they're hurting themselves way more than they're hurting you. Don't expect logic from teenagers!

Give complaining students a couple of extra-credit points or a couple of participation points—whatever your conscience will allow—but let them think you gave something big. Why? Because now they will sing your praises and let the student body know you are fair, reasonable, and good. You will have fewer problems to deal with than if you reacted sternly. But do you compromise deserved grades? No. (For more insight on how extra-credit and participation points work, see Chapters 20 and 22.)

Let's say the student mentioned earlier had a grade of 67.55 percent, and your extra-credit points moved him to 67.85 percent. I can live with

ACTION PLAN

1. When students argue about their grades, find ways to give them what they want without compromising your standards. Offer something like extra-credit or participation points and praise them for their effort and concern. You control the final grade. Make it reflect what is ethical. Participation points and extra credit can make what is wrong right—both to raise grades and to lower grades.

2. Listen to students as though you are on their side. (You are, after all.) Let them know that you are searching for a way to reward them. If you can't—and sometimes you can't—at least they leave feeling heard. And they will tell others of your fairness.

3. Laugh and joke whenever it is appropriate. (Never, of course, make a joke of a student or joke to make light of a student's concern.) Laugh and joke as often as possible. My jokes are terrible, but that does not matter. Kids, unlike adults, are happy with your effort to be funny. Buy a book of jokes if you have to.

4. When you give students something grade-wise, however small, make them feel special. Let them believe you have given so much that they will never ask you for such a favor again. This cuts down on manipulation. When you excuse an assignment, make students feel obliged to do the next assignment as though they will be presenting it on prime-time TV.

5. The temptation to raise your voice is strong and certainly natural, but never raise your voice. Kids don't want to be yelled at any more than you do. And if you

that. Can you? If you think that the scales of justice have been compromised, and you just can't set such a precedent, then pass on this suggestion. But remember that *all grading is subjective*. No matter how good you think your system is, grading is an inherently flawed process.

Here's an example: The five top readers for the AP U.S. history exam sit at a table and read the very same essay. Each reader comes up with a different score. (I have actually seen this happen.) Which one would you like grading your essay?

Yes indeed, the final grade you give your students is just your best guess. The least you can do is acknowledge their efforts and their concern about keeping their grades up.

yell, someone will always misinterpret your message. It is not worth the emotional release.

6. Post this rule in your classroom: "If you have a problem with me or anyone else in this classroom, discuss the problem with me *privately* at an appropriate time. Never criticize, challenge, or complain about anyone in this room *publicly*." Assure students that the rule applies to you, too. This rule is very effective for preventing escalating conflicts and hurt feelings. Explain to your students that you will tolerate no negative discussion in a public setting. Whatever the problem is, most students will just let it go long before they come to you privately.

7. During group work, sit down with each group and just talk with them. Smile and laugh.

8. Show some passion about something besides academics. Talk about your favorite football team or TV show or singer. Ask students about theirs.

9. Be the master of hyperbole. Exaggerate to the point of ridiculousness. Students will love it. For example, say, "This is the greatest essay that I have ever read in my 400 years of teaching!" Or, "Jillian will someday be president of the United States, and when she is, I will be hired as her chief of staff." Or, "Remember, Elvis Presley bought his friends expensive gifts. I prefer automobiles."

CHAPTER 5

Group Therapy, or the Socratic Seminar

For our purposes, let's define the Socratic Seminar as a class discussion on a selected reading or topic. For this discussion, all the students place their desks or chairs in a circle (and a second inner circle, if needed). The Socratic Seminar is "group therapy," in a sense, because it allows the students to examine one another's thought processes, values, backgrounds, and perspectives in a safe way. This type of discussion can help build teamwork, respect, and communication within the classroom. It is one of the most memorable learning activities that a student can engage in during secondary school.

I encourage you to try the Socratic Seminar if you aren't doing it already. You have nothing to lose and great deal to gain—even if your first few attempts go terribly. Don't worry about following the Socratic method just right or whether your questions are truly Socratic in nature.

Perhaps the best way to understand this type of discussion is to read about some actual Socratic Seminars. Following are three examples—seminars focused on a selected reading, a news topic for debate, and a school or class issue. You could try any of these in your own classroom.

Selected Reading

Step one: Make a class set of a selected reading. The reading should be about one-half to one page long and should pertain to your current curriculum or unit objectives. For example, if you are currently studying the U.S. Civil War, make a class set of the Gettysburg Address.

Step two: Create three guiding or starting questions:

1. What is the context for this passage?

2. Why do you think it has become so popular over time?

3. Do you think we have reached the goals implied in the speech? In what ways?

Step three: Set aside five to ten minutes for students to silently read the passage.

Step four: Divide the class into groups of three to five students each to discuss the three questions that you have created. This step is not always needed, but it does create a mini-practice session, which gives some students confidence to express themselves in a larger group.

Step five: Arrange all the students' chairs or desks in a large circle for the whole-class discussion.

Step six: Ask the class your first question and move on with the other questions as you see fit.

Step seven: Guide the discussion by asking questions such as:

- Why do you feel that way?

- How did you reach that conclusion?

- Have you thought about . . . ?

- What if someone responded to you and said . . . ?

- What problems can you see coming up if we fast-forward this logic to its end?

> *The Socratic Seminar is "group therapy," in a sense, because it allows the students to examine one another's thought processes, values, backgrounds, and perspectives in a safe way. This type of discussion can help build teamwork, respect, and communication within the classroom. It is one of the most memorable learning activities that a student can engage in during secondary school.*

Currently Debated News Topic

Step one: Show a video of people debating the topic. For example, if you want to cover the U.S. presidential debates, have students watch the debates in class or as an assignment.

Step two: Create three guiding or starting questions:

1. What issues did you find most interesting?

2. Which candidate answered the question more precisely?

3. Who do you think won the debate? Explain.

Step three: Divide the class into groups of three to five students each to discuss the three questions that you have created (optional).

Socratic Seminars help your students develop critical thinking skills and build relationships. Both are valuable skills in college, work, and life in general. Moreover, Socratic Seminars make your class more interactive and fun.

Step four: Arrange the students' chairs or desks in a circle for the full-class discussion.

Step five: Ask the class your first question and move on with the remaining questions as you see fit.

Step six: Guide the discussion by asking questions such as:

- Why do you feel that way?
- How did you reach that conclusion?
- Have you thought about . . . ?
- What if someone responded to you and said . . . ?
- What problems can you foresee if we fast-forward this logic to its end?

School or Class Issue

Step one: Write a summary of the issue in one page or less. For example, if the class is having an issue with bullying or inappropriate cell phone use, describe the problem and explain why it is a problem.

Step two: Create three guiding or starting questions:

1. What responsibility do you have regarding this issue?

2. Why do people feel justified acting in such a way?

3. What would be a potential solution to the problem? Explain.

Step three: Divide the class into groups of three to five students each to discuss the three questions that you have created (optional).

Step four: Arrange the students' desks or chairs in a circle for the whole-class discussion.

Step five: Ask the class your first question and move on with the rest of the questions as you see fit.

Step six: Guide the discussion by asking questions such as:

- Why do you feel that way?

- How did you reach that conclusion?

- Have you thought about . . . ?

- What if someone responded to you and said . . . ?

- What problems can you predict if we fast-forward this logic to its end?

Besides engaging students more deeply in the curriculum, Socratic Seminars can improve the overall dynamics of your class. The more of these discussions you conduct, the more students will see one another and you as a real person—one whom they might just like. Socratic Seminars help your students develop critical thinking skills and build relationships. Both are valuable skills in college, work, and life in general. Moreover, Socratic Seminars make your class more interactive and fun. I don't use the word *fun* lightly. I think it is overused and misused, and I think the idea of fun is overemphasized in education. But I do believe that Socratic Seminars can make your class more enjoyable in a useful way: they help students want to attend more, listen more, and most importantly, learn more.

ACTION PLAN

1. Attempt a Socratic Seminar early in the year. It is a good way to get to know your students and a good way to start them off with positive attitudes about your class and about you personally.

2. Don't worry about following my instructions perfectly. Trial and error is the best way to establish a routine of Socratic Seminars, because it will give you the opportunity to see what you personally can tolerate and enjoy.

3. Make sure that your selected reading, video, or school issue is interesting.

4. Give the students a handout (see pages 41–42) suggesting questions they can ask or comments they can make, so all feel confident about participating. Don't expect perfection, but you will likely be surprised at your students' ability to think at a higher level.

Don't Know What to Say During a Socratic Seminar?

1. I agree with _____'s thinking on this because . . .

2. I disagree with _____'s thinking on this because . . .

3. I see another possibility here. Consider this . . .

4. To summarize what I hear _____ saying, I would say . . .

5. I think another way of solving this problem would be to . . .

6. _____'s response does not make sense to me because . . .

7. If what _____ says is true, then the next step would be . . .

8. To restate _____'s response in my own words, I would say . . .

9. To add to or clarify the point _____ is making, I would say . . .

10. _____, could you clarify what you meant when you said . . . ?

11. I think that there is another approach that we should consider, and it is . . .

12. I see _____ and _____'s answers to be similar in that . . .

13. I see _____ and _____'s answers to be different in that . . .

14. I just don't see that _____ is true. It is false because . . .

15. I would have to agree with what the text says here: _____. I agree because . . .

16. I would have to say that it is impossible to prove (quote the text) because . . .

17. I interpret the following (quote the text) this way . . .

18. I would say that the following (quote the text) has these implications . . .

19. I think the weakness in the following (quote the text) is . . .

20. I believe the following perspective (describe the perspective) is missing from (quote the text) . . .

21. I would say that (quote the text) is outlining the following viewpoint (describe the viewpoint) . . .

22. Could someone clarify the following for me? (Quote the text.) What I don't understand is . . .

23. _____, could you explain to me how you came to this conclusion?

24. In order draw a conclusion, I think we would need to understand the following . . . (Describe what is missing.)

→

25 I think that we can infer the following from (quote the text) . . .

26 I think that an alternate interpretation to _____'s response is . . .

27 If this were true (quote the text), then I would predict the following . . .

28 _____, how can you say (quote a fellow student) on the one hand and yet believe (quote the same student) . . .

29 The opposing view to _____'s thinking would be . . .

30 I would simplify the following statement (quote the text) by saying . . .

31 I don't think that there is enough information to draw such a conclusion. We still need to know the following (describe what is missing) . . .

32 What if we started with the following assumption? (Describe the assumption.) Would you still feel the same way?

33 What if you were from (describe a different cultural viewpoint)? Would you still take this stand?

34 _____, what if you are wrong about this? How would you justify the damage your choices would cause?

35 To what extent can you attribute your stand on this issue to the viewpoints of your parents?

36 In what ways, _____, do you feel that your friends or upbringing have shaped your view on this matter? I think that you may be influenced in the following ways (describe) . . .

37 I think that _____'s perspective is typical of our generation because I have also heard the following viewpoints expressed (describe the viewpoints) . . .

38 I think that a historian would look back on the perspectives we're offering and give the following interpretation to our thinking (describe the interpretation) . . .

39 I know that my perspective may not be popular, but I think that we are failing to see the following key point (describe the key point) . . .

40 _____, how did you come to feel that way? Your viewpoint does not match your personality in that (describe the contradiction that you see) . . .

CHAPTER 6

AVID Strategies and Why They Work

The Advancement Via Individual Determination (AVID) educational program began in 1980 with one teacher in one school. Over the past four decades, it has grown popular in the United States and elsewhere, involving more than 700,000 students in forty-five states and sixteen other countries. Many districts have embraced the program, or at least its philosophy. The AVID philosophy is simple and powerful. It says that if educators hold students accountable to the highest standards and provide academic and social support, students will rise to the challenge.

What does this mean in practice? AVID employs four main techniques to accomplish these goals:

1. **AVID tutorials twice a week:** These full-period sessions are opportunities for students to receive specific guidance on personal academic challenges. They write their problems or learning challenges on a whiteboard. After that step, their group guides them to the answer in a Socratic manner. The student must then teach the solution to the group.

2. **Organizational and motivational monitoring through constant grade and notebook checks:** When students know teachers are monitoring their work, the results are marvelous. This monitoring is not time-consuming; it's just checking to see that the work is being done.

3. **Team building and group accountability:** These goals are accomplished by both the tutorials and the instructor in the role of academic coach.

4. Use of the Socratic Seminar: The first three strategies provide support and trust. Students and teachers need such a foundation in order to benefit from a Socratic Seminar.

How successful is this approach? Many students echo an expression similar to the following from one of my students: "AVID has become my other parent, getting on me about my grades and keeping me motivated when my hardworking mother can't keep an eye on me. My AVID family keeps me working when I feel like stopping." For more information on the AVID program, see the Recommended Resources on page 189.

The AVID Tutorial

To me, creating a family or team atmosphere is the greatest of all AVID principles. But how, exactly, do you build an AVID-style family or team? Use the AVID elective class tutorial format. Use the Socratic Seminar. Ask about your students' grades. Show personal interest.

The AVID elective class tutorial is ever-evolving, but in simple terms: it's a student-directed, small-group discussion. This discussion consists of a group of five to eight students with their own whiteboard, tutor, and tutorial request form (TRF). (For more information on the TRF, see page 45. For a sample TRF, search online using the term *AVID tutorial request form*.) In the AVID elective class, the tutorial is usually done twice a week. During this time, a college student hired as a tutor guides the students through their homework and the concepts introduced in the classes that they are struggling with. When you re-create this tutorial in your regular class, if you don't have the luxury of college-age tutors, you arrange multiple groups so that in each group, a top academic student is the group leader.

Why am I suggesting a top academic student? Is this fair? When and how do these high-performing students get the academic support that they might need? Those are good questions. It really doesn't have to be the top academic student in every case. However, often the top academic performers are also the most mature, focused, and goal-oriented individuals in your class. They have at least mastered the processes of school at a level other students have not achieved. Selecting top students often requires less training and oversight on your part to get groups working effectively. This strategy is probably best for you in terms of your workload and stress.

But is this strategy fair to the students themselves? I honestly don't know—but I do think it is best for most students in the long run. The tutor is not meant to be a teacher but rather a facilitator who directs the questions and focus of the group toward solving the problem. The leaders of AVID often comment that AVID tutors don't have to be experts, but rather people who can direct a group toward a destination. If you're uncomfortable about always asking the same top students to lead AVID-style groups, the solution is simple: rotate your tutors on a weekly or monthly basis. Remind student tutors that they can get their personal academic struggles addressed by switching roles whenever necessary.

The tutorial plays out something like this in AVID elective classes: Before class begins, every student in the class fills out a TRF. This form, which you can adapt for tutorials in your regular classes, allows students to write two questions each student is struggling with, using Costa's higher-level questioning techniques.* Such questions are conceptual for the most part, not factual. They are not questions that can be answered in a few words, such as "Who is buried in Grant's Tomb?" Math questions are a special case, because by nature math questions are sequential critical thinking problems. They are perfect for AVID tutorials. Moreover, for many students math is the greatest challenge to academic success. They want and need help in math.

When your regular class begins, students get into groups, proceed one by one to their whiteboards, and write their questions for their group to see. The group asks each student a series of questions to guide him or her toward an answer. Before the student can sit down, she must explain the answer back to her group. The group (all students except the tutor) take notes throughout the process, and these notes are put on each individual TRF to be turned in later for a grade.

In a class of forty students (yes, I said forty), as I have had, this kind of attention is sorely needed. Here is a snapshot of a typical tutorial in my classroom. I use AVID tutorials once a week or so.

---

*Educator Arthur Costa's model of thinking and questioning includes three levels of questions. Questions on the first level require students to remember and to show understanding. Questions on the second level require students to use understanding, to examine, and to create. Questions on the third level require students to decide and to support with evidence.

John puts the following question on the whiteboard for his group of eight. "The 1920s were a period of tension between new and changing attitudes on the one hand and traditional values on the other. What led to the tension between old and new, and in what ways was the tension manifested?"

John tells the group that this is the essay he must write in his IB History of the Americas class on Friday. He has never written an essay like this with a score above 60 percent thus far, and he is frustrated and feels stupid. He has always been good at writing essays, but this time he just does not get what the teacher is looking for. "What the heck is going on?" he laments.

> The AVID philosophy is simple and powerful. It says that if educators hold students accountable to the highest standards and provide academic and social support, students will rise to the challenge.

The tutor or student leader makes the first comment: "Well, I don't know much about this either, but the question says that the 1920s were a period of tension between old and new attitudes and values. Maybe we could start by getting out some textbooks from John's class and making a list of old versus new values. Let's look up the 1920s in the text."

At this point all the students except John—who is still standing at the whiteboard—are flipping to the chapter titled "The Roaring Twenties." Student two offers up, "It says here something about flappers."

"I remember all about that," John says. He writes "flappers" on the whiteboard as the other students write on their personal TRFs.

Student three (who is not in John's history class) shouts out, "KKK was active—says on page 327." "Oh, yeah," says John. "We saw this video called *The Birth of a Nation*. I remember the teacher said increasing immigration caused tension."

Student four (who is in John's history class) adds to this, saying, "Yes, I remember that video, too. Mrs. J. said that industrialization had caused tension. I think she was trying to help us on this essay. Let me get my notes out."

Student five says, "I got nothing." The tutor retorts, "What do you mean you got nothing?" "Well, I don't like history," student five says. "So what?" says the tutor. "I don't either, but you will be writing essays like this no matter what."

Student six says, "That's the problem for me. I can't write these essays the way she wants them, even when I know the subject matter." Student seven chimes in with agreement.

The tutor responds, "Well maybe that's what we should talk about: how to write an IB-style essay—no matter what the topic."

John agrees, "Well, I really think that is my problem. I can always find stuff about the 1920s on the Internet, but I don't know what to use or not use."

In what ways did this group help John meet his challenge of preparing for the IB History of the Americas essay? The tutorial helped him in all the following ways, some direct and some indirect:

- Even though he gets very little help with the topic per se, John now knows what his real problem is. It's understanding how to answer the prompt in way that meets the IB standards.

- John discovers that student four has some notes on the essay topic. John now has someone who can help him with the subject matter.

- Students six and seven are in the same boat as John. The tutor can encourage all of them to form a study group outside of class.

- The tutor now knows that John's question is not about content. Rather, his problem is about method. Now the tutor can direct the group toward developing ideas on how to tackle an essay prompt like the one John presented.

- Most importantly, the teacher, after discussing the tutorial with the tutor, realizes that his students need help on how to write an IB essay. He can adapt his lesson plans to the needs of the students.

- All eight of the students in John's tutorial group are feeling safer and more confident about expressing themselves, sharing their academic problems, and asking for help because they are realizing that several other students are having the same problems. Feeling safe enough to ask questions and get help from peers is key to learning. The tutorial format is great at providing a safe venue.

Types of AVID Tutorials

You can use the AVID tutorial format not only in the AVID elective class but also in any regular class. In this section, I'll show how you can apply AVID teaching strategies in various classroom settings.

The AVID-Style Tutorial Before the Test or Essay

Step one: Divide your class into tutorial groups of five to eight students each. The appointed tutor will have students write their questions on whiteboards and discuss them in the manner described previously. These questions can be specific, from your study guide for the test or from an essay prompt.

Step two: Walk around and make sure all the students are engaged in the discussions and are taking notes and offering comments. Before students leave the whiteboard, make sure that they can explain back to their groups the answers to their questions.

AVID-Style Socratic Seminar After Introducing a Concept or to Review a Concept Before a Test

Step one: Arrange the entire class into a large circle (or two) so that everyone has a good view and can freely discuss the topic that you have lectured on.

Step two: Begin the discussion. Let's say your topic is the extent to which Abraham Lincoln's leadership was the reason the Union forces won the American Civil War. Ask, "So, what do you think? How important was Lincoln to final victory?"

Step three: Monitor the discussion and keep it on topic. Call on students who are not speaking. Ask if they agree or disagree with what other students have said.

ACTION PLAN

1. Remember why AVID strategies are worth trying. They create buy-in for you as a teacher and for the content you are teaching. They also help students develop a peer support system.

2. Employ the AVID strategies at various times in the year. Do you have a test coming up? Try an AVID-like tutorial session. Are your students bored with your lessons and developing poor attitudes? Wake them up with an AVID-style Socratic Seminar. Have your students become disorganized in their approach to your work? Require an AVID-style notebook check.

3. Get some portable whiteboards.

4. Once a semester, allow your AVID tutors and/or student tutorial leaders to have a Tutor Appreciation Day with the tutees. This is a party, yes indeed. There is nothing like a good party to build relationships. The students will love you for it and will work harder than ever before. (Please do not dismiss this suggestion without trying it. If you're worried that administrators will think a party is inappropriate or frivolous, consider this: my superintendent and principal crashed one of my Tutor Appreciation Days. They had no complaints at all—especially after they tasted the enchiladas.)

CHAPTER 7

Giving Homework and Classwork Pass/Fail Grades—What?!

Earlier in this book, we discussed the fact that many students copy or otherwise cheat on homework and classwork. One way to address this problem is to give homework that's hard to copy. Another way is to reward students for the knowledge they acquire through homework and classwork—not for the work itself.

Remember that homework and classwork are like a sports team's practice sessions before a big game. The team may practice every day, but none of the work done at practice gets counted in the standings—not directly, anyway. Why? Because only the skills used in the game count. If you are thinking right now, "I know where this is going, and I don't like it," bear with me. Homework and classwork do matter, and they will continue to exist in education. But we need to rethink how we grade this type of work.

How Much Weight Should Classwork and Homework Have in Determining the Final Grade?

Have you ever had students complain to you in the following way? "Ms. Hardgrade, I do all the work in this class, and I still have a C. When I do all the work in all my other classes, I get A's. I like your class, but something is wrong here." What is this student really saying? Isn't it something like this? "I did all the homework and classwork; now where is my A?"

How do you respond? Perhaps you say something like this: "You said that you *do* all the work in this class. Did you really mean to say that you *turn in* all the work for this class? Do you not copy a single thing from any of your friends during advisory class or AVID study hall? Do you not copy and paste anything off the Internet?" (This scenario is for illustrative purposes only. Actual circumstances may dictate a softer or harder approach.)

The student responds, "I do most of the work—really." Let's assume the student is telling the truth. This makes the situation even more interesting. Even if the student is doing most of the work, he or she is not learning much from the effort. Why? Because the student is just jumping through hoops to get the cookie at the end of the obstacle course—the high grade promised as a reward for doing homework and classwork.

Is that what we really want students to earn? Do we want to give them a grade that reflects work or a grade that reflects knowledge and skill? I propose that we want the latter—especially if this student becomes my future heart specialist. I want to know that this doctor did *not* get a medical degree by doing the work, but by knowing the stuff.

Let's get back to the question that leads off this section. How much weight should we give to classwork and homework? I believe we should weight our assignments enough to keep students doing homework and classwork but not enough to make the final grade more about work than about skill and knowledge.

To be exact: I propose that the total points that a student can accumulate in the homework category might make up 5 percent of the student's final grade. I propose the same for classwork. So you may offer twenty homework assignments and forty classwork assignments in a semester, but whether students do them or not affects the final grade only 10 percent—about one letter grade. This means that 90 percent of any student's grade is determined by assessments outside the realm of homework and classwork.

Earning higher grades is too often more about producing a product by any means convenient than it is about learning. If your grading system is about turning in work, students figure out fast that they can check out mentally and save a lot of effort. Doing work does not mean that you have to think or learn—just perform.

Fostering Academic Honesty

Work does not equal knowledge. Please think about this. In the twenty-first century, we must accept the reality that much of the work we receive from students is not completed honestly. This may sound like a broad assumption, but a variety of studies confirm it. Perhaps for individual teachers, however, it would be better to get proof from your students themselves. After all, you need to know what students are thinking and doing. Interview your students. It only takes a few minutes. Many will tell you that they are like machines, producing whatever product you require to get the grade. They might not use those words, but you can read between the lines. And of course, you'll see evidence of this fact when students perform poorly on a test despite having done all the homework and classwork meant to prepare them for it. Although they turned in the work, they gave it little thought. And they made little mental connection between the work they did and the test. (Please note that some students have test anxiety and perform poorly for that reason. Such students as this you will assess using a variety of methods.)

> Do we want to give them a grade that reflects work or a grade that reflects knowledge and skill? I propose that we want the latter—especially if this student becomes my future heart specialist. I want to know that this doctor did not get a medical degree by doing the work, but by knowing the stuff.

Take the time to have a Socratic Seminar or a class discussion on why cheating is unethical. The reasons may seem obvious; why bother? If you do bother, you will be amazed and enlightened. More importantly, your students will know what you expect in your classroom. The confrontations you will avoid by doing this are numerous. You will avoid the painful meeting that comes with parents, administrators, and students when a student is caught cheating.

It is not as easy as telling students that cheating is wrong, and that's that. As educators, we are coming from a mindset that understands cheating as a clear-cut issue. Twenty-first century students, however, do not see cheating as a simple right-or-wrong issue. It is circumstantial, complicated, and ever-changing to them.

What exactly can you say to students or do with them to adjust their concept of academic honesty? I suggest that you should start with a reflective essay. Try an essay prompt like this: "Most adults in this school would consider copying homework cheating. Is this view outdated? Please discuss under what circumstances copying academic work is acceptable. Would you also define the following as cheating: giving classwork answers to your friends, copying and pasting answers from the Web without citing the source, or emailing or texting your friends your finished work to help them out of a problem? Lastly, what are your thoughts as to how academic dishonesty should be handled within the classroom?" If this prompt seems too long for your students, tailor it to your needs.

Give an essay prompt like this during the first week of school. Why? Because you need to know from the start what your students are thinking so that you can make meaningful adjustments before academic honesty becomes an uphill battle.

What adjustments can you make? Start by bridging the distance between your views and students' views. Do not belittle their views or preach to them; rather, act fascinated by their take on the issue. Ask them to enlighten you and tell you how you should be seeing this problem. Use Socratic questioning and logic. Small discussion groups are a specific, safe way to begin. As you walk the room, listening in on the discussions, throw a question into the mix to get them to consider new ideas.

Please remember this key point: a person's values and beliefs should not and probably cannot be changed by just a few thought-provoking lessons. But don't give up. All year long, reinforce the standard of academic honesty—ever so subtly if need be, with side comments and pithy observations. Students will buy what you are selling when they feel you are not judging them but rather are guiding them. As I have suggested often in this book, the greatest rewards in teaching are connected to solving problems like this. Please accept the challenge. It is worth the effort, because you can effect long-term change both academically and otherwise.

Grade Classwork and Homework Once a Week

Let's say that each week you give five homework assignments and five class assignments. At the end of the week, record a grade for homework and a grade for classwork. Do not record these grades every day; you'll drown yourself in paperwork.

Here's an example. If a student did four out of five homework assignments in the first week of the semester, record 4/5 for Homework Week 1. If the student completed three of five classwork assignments, record 3/5 for Classwork Week 1. What about the quality of work? If it is not up to par, don't give a point for it. There: you've just established a pass/fail grading system for homework and classwork.

Remember to have your TA or a student helper grade all homework and classwork. This is just the sort of work you should delegate. It's not complicated, and it doesn't count for much of the final grade. You will not know for sure whether students did their work honestly and thoughtfully until the test, assuming that you test what you have taught and assigned.

The real proof that students have done their assigned work *and learned something by doing it* comes with the assessment. Don't wait too long for the assessment, or you will inadvertently make the homework appear distant and disconnected. We all forget quickly. Students forget homework especially fast. Perhaps you can give short quizzes after three or four homework assignments to keep students honest and productive. As they do the homework, they will pay attention, because they realize a bigger reward—a high quiz grade—is coming. Remember: the work itself, ironically, proves nothing. It simply offers an opportunity to learn and reinforce important concepts. You need to keep your students working, so give them some points along the way to encourage them—but not too many.

ACTION PLAN

1. Don't overvalue homework and classwork's impact on the final grade. Why reward students just for turning in work, regardless of the effort it took or the learning it reflects? Instead, reward the learners, who will prove—by succeeding on the test—that they've done their work honestly.

2. Take the time to have a Socratic Seminar or a class discussion on why cheating is unethical and not in a student's best interest.

3. At the start of the school year, assign the reflective essay outlined in the "Fostering Academic Honesty" section on page 52. It will provide the catalyst for meaningful discussion and a strong opportunity to reinforce academic honesty in your classroom. Don't stop with the essay, the discussion groups, or the Socratic Seminar. Guide students down the path of academic honesty all year long so that your classroom can function fairly and efficiently.

4. Strongly link classwork to the test, and make sure that your students can see that link. For example, if you give homework consisting of five questions, put those five questions on the test.

5. Use a pass/fail system for grading homework and classwork. Set up a system in which homework and classwork combine to make up 10 percent of the grade.

CHAPTER 8

The Boulder Creek Philosophy

When I began my third teaching job at Boulder Creek Academy, an Idaho private school focused on emotional growth, I encountered what I call the Boulder Creek philosophy. At Boulder Creek, if anyone asked me what I taught and I responded, "I teach history," the asker would immediately correct me by saying, "No, you don't. You don't teach history. You teach Patrick Kelley, and you talk about history in class." At first I thought this was a lot of touchy-feely hooey, but in time I changed my mind.

Eventually I came to understand what the philosophy of teaching "myself" means. It means that if I am a history teacher, I as a person and as a teacher cannot be primarily about history. I cannot expect results simply because I know and can explain history. The Boulder Creek philosophy says that students obtain all knowledge and skills first and foremost through people and relationships. In other words, students (and all of us) learn best—and maybe only—if we have a relationship with or attachment to the teacher. So teaching "myself" means that I must establish relationships with students. This isn't a new concept, and not everybody agrees with it. But I think there's some truth to it, because I've seen it play out time and time again during my teaching career. And it's worth discussing, because if you accept this philosophy, its implications are profound for your work as a teacher.

In Chapter 4, we discussed the teacher likeability factor. I mentioned that students often won't work if they don't like the teacher. Conversely, they often *will* work—even in a subject area they claim to hate and be bad at—if they like the teacher. This is a fact we teachers have to live with.

Teaching Yourself Means Learning About Your Students

Now, the thing about teaching yourself is that it's only partly about you. Establishing relationships with students means that you must not only try to be likable and let your students get to know you; you must also learn a great deal about your students. Why? Well, if you don't know your students, then you don't know what parts of your personality, your beliefs, your expectations, or your experiences you should offer them.

Get to know your students during group work or cooperative learning time. Pull up a chair and join a group. Ask every student in the group some nonthreatening personal opinion questions. Give them all A's for talking to you and don't worry if they fail to complete that day's assigned group work.

Another way you can get to know your students is by asking them about their values. For example, you might assume that students by and large have the same values that you have about academic honesty. But do you really know what your students think? Have you asked them? Here's what the best and the brightest in one class believe about the work they do in school. These are the exact words of the top ten students in an honors history class.

> **Student one, aka Mr. Lenient:** "Teachers should not worry about IB students cheating. Occasionally a student will cheat, and I do not disagree with punishments. But all this pressure IB puts into not cheating will eventually get to a student to where he or she *will* cheat. My stand on academic cheating is that it shouldn't be taken seriously."

> **Student two, aka Ms. Regret:** "I will admit to having allowed a friend to copy my homework. And I must say that I do regret it, because friends often tend to take advantage of you and want to keep on copying."

> **Student three, aka Ms. It–Depends:** "When a person is taking a test, it should not be acceptable to cheat, because the person should be prepared. I believe that copying homework is only acceptable when it is only once in a while, but not every day."

Student four, aka Mr. Lazy: "I feel that these situations are not unacceptable. I have copied homework before, but I'm not saying it was right. I also have plagiarized out of pure laziness, not because I wasn't capable of writing it myself."

Student five, aka Ms. Part-Timer: "If you copy maybe once or twice on the homework, as long as it's not copied entirely, then it's fine."

Student six, aka Ms. Enforcer: "It's annoying to see students ditch class intentionally to miss a test, because it is not fair, which is why I love when teachers give a harder test when a student misses it."

Student seven, aka Mr. Conditional: "I see no wrong with copying homework under certain conditions, which are not being able to do the homework because of an unexpected emergency and if a person did not have time do it."

Student eight, aka Ms. Half-and-Half: "Many will say that cheating is unacceptable under any circumstances, while others such as myself beg to differ. I consider cheating on tests wrong, while I have a different opinion on homework."

Student nine, aka Ms. I'm-No-Rat: "I would never help the cheater, but I know I am not going to rat out my classmate or friend. If it doesn't affect me, it's not my problem. They'll suffer later."

Student ten, aka Mr. Rulebreaker: "I know the world isn't fair, and if you think it is, you're in for a rude awakening. So why should we have to follow every little rule down to the dot?"

Academic dishonesty is a prime example of an area in which the Boulder Creek philosophy of modeling good personal ethics can be a game-changer. If you are not prepared to address this subject directly and firmly, then you can expect cheating all year long. Before your students do any work at the start of the school year, find out what they believe and then define academic honesty clearly for them. I attack this issue the first week of school with an assigned essay. I ask, "How do you define academic cheating? In what circumstances can it be justified? What examples of academic dishonesty do you see most often? What do you feel would be a good solution to the problem?" You can tweak this assignment to fit your style and circumstances, but be sure to use the important elements of the previous prompt: getting a feel for students' stand on the issue and finding out how they feel this issue should be addressed. Through this assignment, you can adjust your lesson plans to reach your students on this or any critical issue that you feel is important.

> *Now, the thing about teaching yourself is that it's only partly about you. Establishing relationships with students means that you must not only try to be likable and let your students get to know you; you must also learn a great deal about your students. Why? Well, if you don't know your students, then you don't know what parts of your personality, your beliefs, your expectations, or your experiences you should offer them.*

There's a moral to this story: Don't get so locked into your teaching routine that you fail to learn from your students. And don't be afraid to try new things. Here's another story to illustrate both points.

About twenty years ago I took my second job in the teaching profession. It was in Central Florida. At the time I'd had just three years of teaching experience, all from the Los Angeles School District. I was one of three candidates for the job. The principal who hired me explained why she chose me over the other two.

"The first candidate has fifteen years of experience," she said. "The second has ten years of experience. But you have the most."

"Actually, I have only three years of experience," I replied. "There might have been a typo on my résumé."

"You still have the most experience," she insisted. "The first candidate has one year of experience repeated fifteen times, and the second candidate also has one year of experience—repeated ten times over. You have three years, but each year you got better. (She must have deduced this from the interview.) So you know three times more about teaching than they do."

Now, I think this commentary was just a little too cool for someone to come up with on the spot. I suspect that this principal read those lines in a magazine and decided to use them on me. I think the real reason I was hired was because it was cheaper to hire a rookie. But I played along.

And I do think the principal made a valid point about teaching experience. I agree with her assertion that most teachers have one year of experience or maybe two replayed over and over again. How do we break this cycle and develop as teachers? We can remind ourselves that we are teaching individual students and not just the curriculum. We can teach *ourselves* more than the curriculum. And we can try new things each year.

At the beginning of each school year, try something you have never tried before. For example, most teachers struggle and struggle every year to get students to read the textbook—or just to read, period—outside the classroom. Every year I attempt a new strategy to address this problem. One year I tried quizzes at the start of class. One year I tried quick-write summaries. One year I had students draw political cartoons that summarized their take on the reading. One year I had students write and answer their own quizzes at home based on the reading.

If you don't try new things, you will become a longtime teacher with only one year of experience under your belt. You will be that teacher who teaches the exact same material in the exact same way year after year. You will be a teacher in name, but not a person whom young people will gravitate to, listen to, work for, improve with, and learn from.

Student Personal Statements

When a student submits an application to attend a four-year university, the process usually includes a personal statement. These personal statements are usually 700 to 1,000 words long, and the prompt is often something like "Tell us something about yourself that cannot be seen readily in your GPA, SAT score, or elsewhere in this application." Use personal statements like this as writing assignments. They are best assigned during the first month of school, so you can get to know your students and adjust your perspective and your lesson plans right from the start. Moreover, personal statements will help you create a family atmosphere and prevent discipline problems from starting or festering. (For more on creating a classroom "family," see Chapter 6.)

I think every teacher, administrator, student, politician, and voter should be forced to read about a dozen randomly selected personal statements before making decisions, judgments, assertions, or policy on education or children's issues. In fact, I think the writers should sit down with these people and read their statements out loud. Why? Most people don't know what kids deal with and need on a day-to-day basis. If you'd like to know more, read the following stories. The writers have given me permission to share their stories, but I have changed the names.

Nicky's Story

Have you ever wanted to feel like you were perfect, even if it was just for a second? Have you ever had someone judge you—look for the slightest imperfection? I have, for most of my life.

That was my life at home and on the stage. I did Glitz beauty pageants from the age of eight to fifteen. I won many titles, including national ones. I have 350 crowns, 150 supreme titles, and money prizes. I won all of these things because the judges thought I was perfect, but they only saw what I wanted them to see. I spent so much money trying to cover myself up. Underneath all that makeup, hair, and glitter was anything but perfection.

It took hours of time trying to look like a Barbie doll—plastic, hard, and perfect. But I had a lot of practice being raised the way I was. My life at home caused my imperfections that I had to cover up. Examples are the fake nails to hide my bitten ones, the makeup to hide the evidence of sleepless nights under my eyes, a fake tan to hide all the bruises and marks, and big teased hair that took hours to condition and tons and tons of sparkles.

Walking onstage, I became perfect. I walked slowly, with grace and poise and a fake smile that hurt when I walked offstage, blowing kisses and waving. I felt a rush going through my body like a drug as I tried to get ready for the next segment. Then in front of people onstage again, I was perfect on the outside.

This was my life on a daily basis. All the money I won was not enough to help my mom pay the bills. All the crowns I won were never good enough for my dad to be proud of me and stay home for once. No, I was never good enough. I wasn't perfect to them.

I would sleep in front of my front door on the carpet, with bugs that would bite me and my dad's keys under me, thinking he wouldn't leave and would be there in the morning. But no, he would always choose drugs over me.

Pageants taught me to try my hardest and never give up and also how to act like a mature woman and how to present myself. Through all of this, I learned nothing is ever perfect.

I love Nicky's statement "I was perfect on the outside." It reminds me that in the classroom, the outside is all we see. We teachers don't know what happens to our students when they go home. I was blown away when Nicky read this essay out loud to the class. We were all speechless. In an instant, we all knew why at times she put her head on the desk and would get teary-eyed. I had thought it was just teen drama—until that moment.

Another important thing I learned from this essay was that Nicky can write. I know her English teacher had never seen her write like this. I wondered: how can we teachers tap into such passion academically?

There are many lessons to be learned from Nicky's personal statement, but most importantly, it taught her classmates and I to see her in a different way than we did before. For my part, I am more eager to encourage and be flexible with her. I can't imagine what she has gone through. Can you?

> Most teachers have one year of experience or maybe two replayed over and over again. How do we break this cycle and develop as teachers? We can remind ourselves that we are teaching individual students and not just the curriculum. We can teach **ourselves** more than the curriculum. And we can try new things each year.

In practical terms, I now have some tools to motivate Nicky, because I know a little bit about her. I now know why she is discouraged at times, and I can work with that. When she sees that I understand and care, she will be less likely to ignore my advice. She will not be able to say to me, "You just don't know what I am going through." In fact, everyone in class can be more supportive and help create a safer environment. It is true that it takes a village to raise a child. This child doesn't have much of a village at home, so I am forming a village at school.

Brianna's Story

I entered the foster care system at the age of seven and bounced from home to home, family to family. I learned how to adapt and how to keep myself emotionally detached in order to survive. The injustices that I observed swirling around me while in the system pushed me into the realization that I was the only one that could save me. I knew that my situation would not last forever, and I decided that I would do everything I could to better the system so that no other child need endure unnecessary hardships. My foster care experiences actually ended up fostering my interest in the legal field, especially family law.

School was the environment I chose in which to submerge myself. Considered by some a prison, school to me was an escape. Those hallways of solace embraced me in their cocoon, giving me leave and comfort from my everyday miseries.

Although I am still enduring a life of foster care, although my trials have yet to end, although I am still trying to break the stereotypical mold of the American foster child, I am learning to let myself trust people—maybe people actually do care!

After reading this essay aloud, Brianna told the class that she was committed to someday becoming a lawyer, just as she'd said in her personal statement. Brianna had a 3.7 GPA. But her intellect—emotionally and otherwise—far exceeds her GPA or her SAT or ACT score.

Timothy's Story

My parents decided on fifty-fifty custody when they divorced, which means my sister and I spend half our time with Mom and half our time with Dad. We switch houses every Friday. This has stuck for our entire childhoods.

Over the years my parents developed two very different households. In fact, I would go as far as calling them complete opposites. My dad got remarried to a very conservative Christian woman, and my mom is dating (and living with) an ex–Hell's Angel.

The two homes could not be any more different, just like the people who occupy them. My dad's house is, well, very Christian and conservative. My dad and stepmom are not very accepting of anything out of the ordinary. They live in a large tract home that is never anything but spotlessly clean. My dad and stepmom attend church every Sunday and are frankly quite boring.

My mom's house, however, is the complete opposite. It is a custom-built, contemporary, open-concept, nontraditional home. My mom and her boyfriend are anything but ordinary. They decorated the house with eclectic décor that ranges from prison art to industrial art to a giant stuffed buffalo head in the dining room. They are very liberal, open-minded people and want my sister and me to feel free to talk about anything.

Growing up in these very different households is anything but easy. I have to alter my attitude and personality to accommodate whichever house I am currently at. When I am at my dad's, I generally stay quiet, afraid of being judged or ridiculed for any comment I make that doesn't closely follow their beliefs, especially politics.

My mother and her boyfriend provide a safe haven where I can talk about anything without being judged. Even if they disagree with me, they will explain why they disagree but will ultimately leave it up to me to decide.

Growing up in these two households is not all bad. It allows me to experience and understand different types of people. I am lucky enough to be exposed to two perspectives. Divorce is a horrible experience, but sometimes good can come out of it.

What do you think about Timothy's experience? Sometimes it is easy to forget that the student we see at school is piloting a nuclear submarine at home. Hearing, reading, and reminding ourselves of the difficult dynamics students face in their domestic settings better equips us to see the student and not just the subject. For example, when students come to me—as they often do—saying that they just cannot cope because of their home lives, I can pull out Timothy's story and remind the overwhelmed student (and myself) of how Timothy copes with his confusion.

Samantha's Story

A day that I cannot shake from my memory, the day I was taken away from my family, was the start of all of my life lessons. I was taken away when I was five years old. I grew up being tossed around from home to home to whoever wanted me. There soon came a court date, which I saw as my escape, because I thought I was going back with my family. But as you all probably know, it did not happen like that—not even close. I had to wait for my parents to complete drug and alcohol classes and parenting classes before I could go back.

After many years of court dates, hoping to go home with my family, I always left the room throwing myself on the ground. Every court date, I entered the room hoping that this might be my lucky break. But every time, that hope quickly disappeared.

When I was twelve, I was finally placed at home with my family. But soon—a little too soon for my taste—my family fell apart. My dad went back to drugs, alcohol, all those things. I stayed stuck in foster care, waiting for him to get himself together.

This whole experience that is my childhood has made me a strong individual.

Do you have a Samantha in your classroom? Perhaps you have several. Many students are not only foster kids but also have someone in their family struggling with alcohol or drugs. We know that such drama changes their view of schoolwork. How do we guide them to separate home life from school life? It helps when they can see that other students have successfully done so. After Samantha read this story, so many kids related with it that we had her read a longer version of it to most of the faculty at the next professional development session. It was powerful. I saw men crying. She was so pleased with her-

> *Remember that the reward for teaching is the personal relationships you create, not the lesson plans. So put relationships first.*

self that her GPA jumped from 2.7 to 3.5 in just four weeks! Was that due to her efforts? Did her teachers see her differently? I think the answer to both questions is yes.

Lucy's Story

I kept trying to push the dog away so I could go into the house, but suddenly my whole head was in the dog's mouth. I couldn't see anything but blackness, and I could only smell the dog's awful breath. Once I screamed for help, everyone was in a panic mode, and my dad pulled the dog's mouth away from my face.

Fast-forward to a year later, when I started elementary school: I was so excited for my first day until a little girl I had never met before asked me what was on my face. I did not know how to answer the question, because my parents would always answer for me. Before I knew it, some of the kids started teasing me and calling me names, like scarface.

One of the skills I learned at a young age was how to take criticism. Now I can handle any insults or remarks that come my way. And since I did not talk a lot in school, I was able to observe other kids around me and notice the mistakes they were making. It caused me to become more aware of what was really important in school.

Now that I am older, I realize that having scars on my face has been a privilege, because it allowed me to grow up quickly and become stronger emotionally and intellectually. Since I am of the age to get my scars surgically removed now, my parents are asking me almost every day if I want to remove them. But I always say that I wouldn't like to get rid of my scars, because they have been a part of my life for twelve years.

Can you imagine what it must be like as a teenager to walk around with a big scar on your face? Image is so important to young people. Reminding ourselves of this fact is important to us as teachers. Lucy teaches us that it is okay to carry our scars as badges of personal growth. Making individuality safe in your classroom is a skill with rewards that are both tangible and intangible. Lucy was a prime target for potential bullying, but because of the lessons she learned in elementary school, she was not bullied in high school. She is a great object lesson for all of us.

How Do These Stories Apply to Teaching?

Now that you have read several personal statements, I hope you can see clearly that knowing the young people you are teaching is essential to surviving, enjoying, and improving as an educator. Your students have compelling stories. They have stories that can refresh and challenge and change your attitude about why you are teaching. They have stories that can motivate their peers to listen and work in your class. They have stories that need to be told.

Sharing these stories provides great opportunities to praise and validate the experiences young people have, to celebrate the obstacles that they have overcome, and to make suggestions as to how they can build on these unique experiences. The sharing process teaches students that they matter to you. Once they believe that, they will be more willing to listen to you all year long.

Reading personal statements in a book is only a fraction as powerful as it is to hear them read aloud by the authors to a class, with all the emotion right out there for all to see—raw and real. Doing this is going to require a couple of days of prep work for younger or less mature students—especially middle school students. Prepare them by reading a sample personal statement from someone who is not a member of the class. This is a safe way to start. Use the five personal statements on pages 61–66. The comments that follow the story will help you develop the discussion with your students. Model how to comment on the story. If, after this modeling session, students still demonstrate a lack of maturity, then wait until they are ready to share personal statements.

I believe you will find that in most cases, your students will rise to the challenge, because they love a lesson like this. Middle school students are more interested in who their peers are than who their parents are. And I have noticed that all tendencies toward bullying in my class end after this lesson is complete.

One of my students attending a college fair held in a huge civic center in Ontario, California, walked up to an admissions officer and asked, "Why don't you have the personal statements read out loud?" "Oh, don't worry; we read them," said the officer. The student replied, "You may read them, but that is not the same as having them read aloud." This kid, unlike the admissions officer, knew just how important it is for educators to know their students as well as possible.

ACTION PLAN

1. To maximize learning, you must make an effort to know your students and to let them know you as a person. You can do this by pulling up a chair and joining a group during cooperative learning times.

2. During the first month of class, find out what your students believe about cheating and teach them the meaning of academic honesty. Use the essay prompt in this chapter to accomplish this goal.

3. Take a few days to learn students' personal stories. This will help you know just how you should teach the standards to them and will motivate them to listen to you with greater zeal and respect.

4. Remember that the reward for teaching is the personal relationships you create, not the lesson plans. So put relationships first.

CHAPTER 9
Classroom Management

Of all topics in the field of education, perhaps none is discussed more often than classroom management. The turnover rate is high for teachers in the first few years of teaching, and I think it is safe to say that in almost every case, part of the reason is the frustration teachers experience while trying to logically and effectively manage their classes under impossible conditions.

Twentieth-century comedy writer and teacher Donald D. Quinn described these conditions: "If a doctor, lawyer, or dentist had forty people in his office at one time, all of whom had different needs, and some of whom didn't want to be there and were causing trouble, and . . . without assistance, had to treat them all with professional excellence for nine months, then he might have some conception of the classroom teacher's job." This quote addresses the most challenging and important component of classroom management: managing student behavior. Classroom management includes other components, too, such as managing lesson plans, managing the grading and recording of student work, and managing communication with families, administrators, and other teachers. But in this chapter, we'll focus on student behavior.

Student behavior, among all the aspects of classroom management, is the one that usually makes or breaks a teacher. How can you manage student behavior to maximize learning? Your success is largely contingent on developing coping strategies.

Notice that I did not say *management* strategies. Why? Because humans are unpredictable and often irrational, especially during the teenage years, so you cannot expect to manage student behavior. You can only manage your reaction to it, or how you cope with it. Moreover, all teachers are different. A situation that one teacher considers to be under control or managed, another might judge to be absolute pandemonium. For example, I might walk into Mr. Laidback's class and see students wandering and talking loudly, desks everywhere, you name it. I might think that this guy has no classroom management skills, while he feels that he has things under control and that learning is moving along as planned.

I—and perhaps you—could never handle such a scene, but Mr. Laidback can. Why? Maybe he can tolerate a level of teenage energy that makes others uncomfortable. Or perhaps more positive things are happening in that classroom than meet the eye. Is Mr. Laidback teaching anything in this environment? Evidently, yes. When asked, most of his students say that they believe they are learning, and they support their assertions with specifics. Mr. Laidback's student test scores are as high as mine, and his stress level seems to be lower.

> Student behavior, among all the aspects of classroom management, is the one that usually makes or breaks a teacher. How can you manage student behavior to maximize learning? Your success is largely contingent on developing coping strategies.

Mr. Laidback has found a way to cope with student behavior and manage his classroom that works for him. Some teachers may believe that kids can learn only in a quiet, controlled setting, but both Mr. Laidback's experience and the research evidence suggest otherwise. Students can learn in a variety of settings and with a variety of approaches. That's why we can't judge classroom management by the amount of activity we see or noise we hear in the classroom. That's also why there is no one-size-fits-all magic formula for classroom discipline.

Engaging Students—What Works?

We have all heard the buzzwords *on task*, *engaged*, *actively involved*, *cognitively processing*, and others. Whichever term you choose, they all express the same idea. That idea describes our ultimate goal in a nutshell: to get students involved in activities that promote learning.

How can you get your students' attention from the start and keep it going throughout a lesson? Well, it helps to understand the typical reasons students engage in schoolwork. Your students will choose to engage for a number of reasons. These reasons have little to do with your discipline strategy and a lot to do with you asserting the best of your personality without fear. (For more on that topic, see Chapter 4.) Here are some common reasons why students engage:

- Your enthusiasm for the subject intrigues them. They wonder, "Why is he so passionate?" They are curious.

- They feel they have no choice but to listen to you, because they find you interesting, funny, or unusual. They don't want to miss the next laugh or be unable to make fun of you later with their friends.

- They know that if they don't pay attention to you, it could be embarrassing, because you keep asking questions that require students to have a clue.

- They don't want you to hassle them; they know that you are watching and irritating kids who slack off.

- They care about their grade, and they've noticed that you reward good behavior and participation.

- You are known as fair and respectful throughout the school. If they act otherwise toward you, it won't go over well with their friends or a vice principal.

- You don't lose your temper and you never let up. There's no point in fighting you, because you never react with anger—just with long, boring lectures.

- They find your lectures boring, but your group work is fun. If students make a stink during the lecture, they'll prolong it and irritate their friends.

- You never discuss problems publicly, so there is no point in causing a problem to get attention. You just step into the hallway with trouble-makers, and all the attention you give them goes unseen by others.

- Your consequences are consistent. You don't compromise or negotiate, so challenging you is a waste of time.

Engaging Students by Managing Your Own Behavior

You might have picked out a common theme in the list on page 70. Classroom management is not just about student behavior—it's about teacher behavior, too. Here are some tips for managing your own behavior in a way that will encourage students to manage theirs:

- State your rules and the consequences for breaking them as soon as possible. Enforce the rules using the stated consequences without emotion. Don't change the consequences.

- Be consistent with all your students. Show no appearance of favor or laziness in your actions.

- Develop a personality with some quirks that make you likable. Ham it up often. Tell stories or jokes. Work on your storytelling skills.

- Never lose your temper in public.

- Don't threaten; just act. Do not warn and then warn some more. This just undermines the effectiveness of your rules and consequences.

> Humans are unpredictable and often irrational, especially during the teenage years, so you cannot expect to manage student behavior. You can only manage your reaction to it, or how you cope with it.

- Don't discuss the behavior of one student with the whole class, even if you think you are not revealing the student's identity. This is unethical.

- Don't generalize. For example, don't say, "You were just terrible with the substitute." Instead, describe the specific undesirable behavior or infraction.

- Don't punish the group for the misdeeds of one or a few.

- Work on the introductions to your lessons so that you grab your students' attention from the start.

- Praise students often, with specificity and sincerity.

- When you need to criticize students, do so with purpose and deep respect. Never show unkindness or lack of self-control—no matter what.

Your reputation eventually will speak volumes about your classroom management skills. And someday you will feel that you have mastered this aspect of teaching—but then the unexpected will happen. Here's a little story to illustrate that. This story shows it's possible to be likable while also being firm and consistent.

One day I was talking with a couple of students, and I thought I smelled smoke—from a fire, not someone smoking. I said so. Things got really quiet.

I looked around and there was a student we'll call Sam with a cigarette lighter, a pencil, a marshmallow, and a chocolate bar. He was making s'mores in the third row. They looked quite good. They began to smell nice. But I was afraid the fire alarm was about to go off. How would I explain this one to administration?

> *Classroom management is not just about student behavior—it's about teacher behavior, too.*

I looked Sam in the eye. He looked me in the eye. Everyone in class took a deep breath. Sam smiled at me. I tried as hard as I could not to smile or laugh, then I looked away.

A few kids were smiling at me but not speaking. I tried not to look at them. They made funny sounds. I looked away again. I looked back at Sam. He offered me the first bite. That's when I lost it and broke into laughter. There was a collective sigh of relief. I still wrote Sam up, of course. It was my first referral in years.

Later, I heard that the vice principals, the secretary, and other office personnel also laughed. It was a funny scene, and there's no getting around that fact. I am glad that I laughed. I could have launched into an angry fit, but laughter was a better choice for classroom management. Thanks to my laughter, I became human to my students that day—just in case some of them had been wondering. And that is the bottom line. A human teacher who's willing to laugh at a ridiculous situation is a likable teacher, one for whom students are willing to work.

A Note on Discipline Referrals

Almost any veteran middle or high school teacher will tell you that writing kids up and sending them out of class is not a pragmatic solution in the long run. In fact, doing so may bias the administration against you. When administrators see a teacher send out a student, they assume that on some level, the problem is the teacher's fault. It is in your best interest to avoid taking this risk. Moreover, if your referrals are few and far between, then the action that administrators will take on your behalf will be commensurate to the rarity and intensity of your classroom management requests. Finally, once your reputation starts down a pathway, it takes a hurricane to blow it back on course. Let your reputation be that of a low-maintenance educator who has a firm handle on discipline.

The Two Best Classroom Rules

For many years, I have been searching for the absolute best classroom rules on the planet. I have seen thousands of posted rules. Here are the two most effective, in my estimation.

Rule One

Do not publicly criticize, challenge, or argue with anyone in this class. If you have a problem with someone in this room, discuss the matter privately with me at an appropriate time.

This is the number one effective rule because it helps you simplify your management task from convincing thirty to forty students that your actions are justified down to convincing just one. In addition, you help the student save face. When you make a problem private, the teen's ego is no longer at stake, and the student feels no pressure to respond publicly. Moreover, the moment you show your students that only one person will be seeing any attention-getting performances they might conjure up, then at that precise moment, you have managed the greatest challenge of student misbehavior. You have fulfilled the human need for recognition, but you have not let this need create new problems for you, because you have managed the settings in which validation will be offered.

You are going to love this rule. I have seen it work for twenty-five years without failure. Now, how do you put this rule into practice?

At the beginning of the year, explain to your students that in any situation where humans interact, friction will occur. This is just the nature of being human and living with other humans. We get on one another's nerves, and conflict results. But we can all agree from the start to handle these conflicts respectfully. If two people have a problem, they do not need to air their dirty laundry in front of the group. It doesn't solve anything.

For my students, I always break down the concepts in this rule. I start with the word *publicly*. What does that mean? Why is it unwise to discuss personal problems publicly? I also break down the word *criticize*. How can you criticize someone indirectly? How can you challenge someone without directly saying something out loud? Can you challenge without words? How? Can you criticize without words? How? I discuss other important concepts, too. For example, what is an argument? Does your tone of voice matter? What is attitude? Who determines an appropriate time to discuss a problem privately? What is not an appropriate time? Why? What is respect? How is respect involved with selecting an appropriate time? Why is privacy so important in solving personal disputes that arise in a classroom? Do young people act differently in front of their peers? Why?

This is a great Socratic Seminar topic. I highly recommend that you use the above questions, along with some specific examples that have happened in your class in the past, as a first-week-of-school discussion.

Rule Two

When the teacher is talking, remain silent and face the teacher.

This rule works well for at least two important reasons. Firstly, it is almost impossible to teach well if your mind is on the fact that some of your students are not fully engaged. If two or three students are making noise, you have to stop what you are doing and fix the problem. Boy, does that get old! You can teach much more effectively if this type of distraction stops. Secondly, many people need a calm, peaceful environment in order to concentrate on a speaker.

How do you put this rule into practice? When I introduce this rule, I start discussing it by focusing on the words *remain silent*. I explain to my students that in a public setting, such as during a lecture or instructions, respect requires silence so that everyone in the room, regardless of personal challenges, can concentrate on what is being said. Talking or sighing or fidgeting or noise of any kind is disrespectful and often distracting.

Next I break down the idea of facing the teacher. This is a good time to discuss body language. Students have a tendency to use body language that indicates they are about to pounce on a side conversation with a neighbor or friend the second the teacher blinks too long. I love to illustrate this for them with over-the-top physical demonstrations of how students show their true colors with their body language. They find these antics quite funny. Sometimes I get so carried away that I can't stop laughing myself. They get scared for me, because when I laugh too hard, I start to cry. But they love every minute of it, and it makes an unforgettable impression that lasts an entire year. Sometimes students will ask for a repeat performance, and I am almost always willing to give one because it cements the rule quite nicely.

It is important to remember that students will always challenge you. They will always criticize you. They will always try to argue with you. But if they do not do this publicly, taking time away from instruction and escalating the issues, your student behavior challenges will be far fewer. If students attempt to do so, but you restate your rule and discuss it with them at an appropriate time, by the time that time arrives—even if it is just five minutes later—most aspects of the problem will no longer exist. In the case that they do still exist, the extra five minutes will do wonders for the tone, control, and logic of the situation.

ACTION PLAN

1. Be consistent with your rules and consequences.

2. Keep your reactions under control.

3. Be prepared with engaging lessons.

4. Be likable and share your humor or your passion.

5. Don't take yourself too seriously.

6. Don't punish the many for the misdeeds of the few.

7. Don't discuss dirty laundry publicly.

8. Show that you really like your students and care about them on a personal level.

9. Use positive reinforcement; negative rarely works.

10. Have fun or try something else as a profession, because students can smell contempt and sense frustration before any words leave your mouth.

CHAPTER 10

Planning Lessons and Charting Progress

If your lesson plans failed last year, would you use them again this year without any modification? Some teachers do exactly that for various reasons. Perhaps they plan lessons the same way from year to year because this is a routine that works for them. They are striving for simplicity and familiarity. Or perhaps they just don't know whether their lesson plans have succeeded or failed. Without a solid answer to that question, why go through the effort to change?

Are good standardized test scores a sufficient measurement of successful lesson plans? To some extent they are. But test scores tell only part of the story. Kids who love learning and are motivated to be lifelong learners tell the rest of the story. How can we use lesson plans to bundle a love of learning in with good test scores? We do that by creating lessons that not only have clearly defined objectives, but also employ the power of competition.

Planning Lessons: The Power of the Objective

Lesson planning is a topic as wide as the Grand Canyon. I bet there are more lesson-planning templates in our schools than there are students. I'm sure some teachers do use such templates—complete with objectives, standards, assessments, activities, independent practice, modeling, group practice, homework, and remedial work. Yet I know of no veteran teachers who use formal ones, except to post in their classrooms. Whether our lesson-planning approach is formal or informal, for most of us the following three elements are in play:

1. What are the topics (written as behavioral objectives) that I must cover?

2. Considering the materials available to me, what are the best items and activities to use? Do I have videos? Do I have handouts? Do I have projects? Do I have class discussion topics? What worked last year, and what did not work?

3. How will I evaluate what my students have learned?

With this common reality in mind, I propose a three-step lesson-planning strategy. Not the beloved five-step method. Not seven steps or even the nine steps I mentioned before. Just three.

Step one: Come up with the best behavioral objective that you can. Word it carefully and clearly. Make sure that it connects to the state standards. Notice that I used the term *behavioral objective*. This is the only term I've learned in the thirty or so education classes I've taken over the years that has made a lasting impression on me. Behavioral objectives are the things we teachers are trying to teach our students to think and do. They are actions that students can do after the lesson that they could not do before the lesson. (Or perhaps students can do *better* after the lesson at whatever we are trying to teach them.) We can express behavioral objectives in language such as: "discuss in writing . . . ," "orally explain . . . ," "orally evaluate . . . ," "tell the story of . . . ," "complete the equation . . . ," "analyze the film by writing an essay that . . . ," "critique the art by identifying on paper the following . . . ," and so on. Lessons with behavioral objectives affect student behavior, and this behavioral change should be measurable. If we teach without sound, measurable objectives, little learning takes place in most cases.

> Are good standardized test scores a sufficient measurement of successful lesson plans? To some extent they are. But test scores tell only part of the story.

For example, your objective might be "Students will analyze the causes of the U.S. Civil War, and this will be measured by a four-page in-class essay that will be graded according to the IB rubric for essays." Some sticklers will point out that this objective is missing information on how many students you expect to meet this objective and your plans for remediation and reteaching. I say let's be real. If you include all that for every lesson, you will never get past the first chapter of your text, and you'll drive most of your students crazy. Of course, you'll try to do all those things as you teach, but you don't need to write it all out on a form; it's too time-consuming.

Behavioral objectives are the things we teachers are trying to teach our students to think and do. They are actions that students can do after the lesson that they could not do before the lesson.

Step two: Prepare what you will say to explain the objective and how you will have the kids examine the topic. I think the big question here ought to be "What activities actually help kids meet the behavioral objectives, and what activities are just fluff?" Fluff has its place at times, but it shouldn't make up the bulk of any lesson. If what kids are doing in class bears little resemblance to what we want them to do on a test or an essay, we should think twice about the activity.

For the sample objective on the Civil War, your activities could be many. They might include a movie on the causes of the Civil War, a group discussion on the ills of slavery versus the importance of states' rights, a group practice essay, a worksheet on the causes of the Civil War, ten lectures, and two quick writes (see page 108 for more about quick writes).

Step three: Assess what your students have learned or achieved from the lesson. The assessment should mimic the objective exactly or almost exactly. For the sample objective on the Civil War, then, your assessment should be a four-page in-class essay analyzing the causes of the Civil War, graded according to the IB rubric for essays.

Charting Progress: The Power of Competition

Just three steps can simplify lesson planning into a manageable, effective process:

1. Behavioral objective that is clear and measurable

2. Activities directly related to the objective

3. Assessment in the same wording as the objective

Simple and effective lesson plans point the way to higher test scores. Now let's add one more ingredient to the recipe of successful lesson planning: competition.

Only a few times in my career have I been truly blown away by the effectiveness of a certain technique in education. One of these techniques is using the power of competition to transform class dynamics and achieve success. Here's what happened.

One year we did a cookie dough fundraiser in the AVID program. I'll be honest: I hate fundraisers. The cookie dough vendor seemed to hate fundraisers, too. It was no surprise when eighty AVID students sold exactly eighty tubs of delectable dough, bringing in precious little dough for our program. But the next year, a new cookie dough vendor seemed to like this doughy deal quite a bit more. She hung a chart in my room to monitor the students' sweet progress. This time, the same number of students sold 300 tubs of cookie dough. I did nothing different from the previous year. The chart did all the work! The difference in result was huge, and the cause was obvious.

> Charting works because many students love competition. To tap this enthusiasm, we should chart attendance, grades, attitudes, test scores, or whatever else needs improvement.

This got me thinking. I recalled that I had charted my students' progress before over the years, and I'd seen similar incredible results. I stopped charting when the folks in administration explained to me that I could not post the students' real names on the charts. I guess they were trying to protect egos and privacy.

I didn't think of the following solution back then, but now I know it works: I let the kids make up secret names that only they and I know. Charting progress is powerful, and I don't want to miss the opportunity to use it.

Charting works because many students love competition. To tap this enthusiasm, we should chart attendance, grades, attitudes, test scores, or whatever else needs improvement. As with any technique, the novelty of competition wears off if we overuse it. So it's important to use it judiciously. Change charts often to refresh the novelty and to give different students the recognition and glory they long for. Give out awards and certificates. Make sure your certificates look professional and read well, or they'll be worthless or even damaging—and you'll be a laughingstock. Be ceremonial in your presentation. Act as though an award-winning kid has just won an Oscar. Take the achievement seriously, but also show humor if you can, and have some fun. Kids—even high school students—just love this stuff!

By the way, you'll be surprised at how parents react to achievement charts. Many will look at these charts as if they are trying to figure out their own 401k plan. They will push their kids to make the cut.

And remember: charting is clerical work, not teaching. Have a TA or student helper record achievements on your classroom chart(s). You can have this person design and administer the awards or certificates, too.

ACTION PLAN

1. Use the three-step lesson plan described in this chapter. Avoid lesson plan templates, which may contain more words than the U.S. Constitution and take more time than standing in line at the Department of Motor Vehicles.

2. Assess your objective, not the subject matter. When you create the objective, you have also created the test—or vice versa.

3. Select activities that relate directly to the objective. Students need the correct practice before the assessment.

4. Use bar graphs and pie charts to record student achievements. These types of charts are easy for most students and administrators to read and understand.

5. Decorate your charts with art. Pretty charts are more enticing.

6. Hype the charts each day. Put them in a prominent place, such as on the door or the whiteboard.

7. Give out certificates to recognize top achievers in all categories.

CHAPTER 11

Imparting Knowledge vs. Producing a Product

Thousands of students in the United States—and around the world, I suppose—have high GPAs but little knowledge of the subject matter the A's on their transcripts say they've mastered. Imagine if this happened in medical school. Who would want a doctor who aced medical school but knows little about medicine?

Of course, this disconnect between grades and knowledge is nothing new. There have always been some students who cheat their way to the top of the class. However, some aspects of this problem have changed. Students are better at cheating now, and they have more ways of doing it than ever before. With modern technology, students can copy massive amounts of material. What is more: the current difficult economic climate makes some students more motivated to cheat. They feel they must succeed at any cost. That's why it's important for teachers to remember that if an assignment can be copied, it probably will be. Math homework is shared during science class. History is copied during algebra. Science homework is cut and pasted from the Web. The assigned work is Googled, emailed, font-changed, Yahooed, and Wikipediafied—simply because it can be.

This means that many students are going through the system mastering the products (assignments) required of them without learning much about the concepts these assignments are supposed to help them learn. For example, how many AP students fail miserably at the AP U.S. history exam despite having an A in the class? A lot of them. If you visit the College Board's official website, you will notice that historically the pass rate is in the neighborhood of 51 percent. Of the 49 percent who fail, how many achieved an A in the class? Official stats on this are not available, but we do know that the average GPAs of AP students are high. In other words, they must be scoring well in their AP classes in order to get grades that sustain their high GPAs. Why do these students fail the AP exam? One big reason: they know how to follow the teacher's system to get good grades, but they're just churning out products; they're not learning what they need to know about the subject matter.

Grade inflation is a related problem. Grade inflation is the tendency to give higher grades for work that would have earned lower grades in the past. It has been well documented in the United States, and I fear it will continue to grow.

Grade inflation presents a big problem for students, teachers, parents, schools, and society. Because of grade inflation, these long-held indicators of student performance are losing their meaning. It is becoming very difficult to use grades to evaluate, represent, and interpret student performance. Here's an example to illustrate the problem: Ms. Jackson's Algebra I class receives twenty-five A's, whereas Ms. Yamota's Algebra I class receives just three A's. Obviously, an A in Ms. Yamota's class has a different meaning than an A has in Ms. Jackson's class. Meanwhile, the standardized test scores show that both classes have mastered the subject matter on an equally poor level.

> Many students are going through the system mastering the products (assignments) required of them without learning much about the concepts these assignments are supposed to help them learn.

What causes grade inflation? It's easy to point a finger at teachers, but the real cause lies in educational policies and societal pressures to which teachers must conform.

Let's talk about those policies and pressures a bit. Teachers get flak from everyone if their students have low grades. Low grades make students look bad. They also make parents, teachers, principals, and schools look bad. Angry or embarrassed students claim injustice and badger counselors to be moved into another class. Parents want their kids placed somewhere else "so they can succeed." Principals field unpleasant parental phone calls. Teachers get scrutinized by administrators.

Also, giving low grades makes teaching more difficult. Students who think that you are unfair are less inclined to listen and work hard in your class. They measure fairness, of course, by how easy you grade your students and how much work you give. Where students are concerned, a teacher's reputation is paramount. Being a hard grader is not a helpful reputation to have.

The Problem with Fun

Adding to this problem is the fact that many modern students believe teachers should make learning fun. Following is a list of common student expectations and attitudes. These ideas directly and indirectly discourage teachers from applying academic rigor in their classrooms. They tug at teachers' emotions and derail the proper planning of constructive lessons.

- A teacher should be a great entertainer.

- A teacher should be lively.

- A teacher should make learning hands-on.

- A teacher should address my learning modality and preferences.

- A teacher should use modern technology.

- A teacher should be funny.

- A teacher should not give hard tests.

- A teacher should not assign essays.

- A teacher should understand that I have other homework.

- A teacher should know that I do not do well on certain kinds of tests.

It's true that we should try to teach in a way that intrigues and motivates students—but not at all costs. Making lessons fun is less important than improving student skills or increasing academic development. Learning and improving is the true fun that happens in a classroom. Fun should not mean entertainment or avoiding commitment and hard work.

In an effort to accommodate bored students, educators often feel pressured to be entertainers rather than teachers. This pressure can result in lessons with lots of bells and whistles that earn praise from administrators, parents, and students—but from which, in the end, students learn very little.

Do students ever have to pay the price for producing without learning? Yes, they pay it first during high-stakes testing. For example, a student who makes an elaborate volcano with a remote control has a lot of fun and makes an impressive product, but doesn't learn much about geology. A group of kids who spend thirty hours creating a beautiful video on the signing of the Declaration of Independence love the experience, but it doesn't help them much on the state standardized history test. A whole class spends twenty hours on a Treaty of Versailles simulation. They have a blast, and they like the teacher now. But the teacher can't measure much profit beyond that. Mr. Reasonable plays math bingo with his class every Friday for one hour. He is the most popular and most highly regarded math teacher in the school. But the hours spent on games contribute few—if any—points to his students' AP exam scores.

> *Making lessons fun is less important than improving student skills or increasing academic development. Learning and improving is the true fun that happens in a classroom. Fun should not mean entertainment or avoiding commitment and hard work.*

Students pay the price again in college. Remember that even though schools may play to students' strengths if they can, colleges generally won't. They don't care if students don't like essays. They don't care if students second-guess themselves on multiple-choice tests. They don't care that students love to play Jeopardy when it is time to review material. They don't care if students can sing and dance in a cool skit on the Salem witch trials. They do care if students can write, analyze, discuss, and demonstrate on paper some knowledge of the subject at hand. Colleges want students to prove that they can think.

What does this mean for you personally? It means that you shouldn't give in to the pressure to entertain your students. Teach them instead. Tell your students that you care about their success, and that simply means they must face reality. Be frank with your students. Convince them that they can develop the skills they need to learn outside their preferred modalities. Explain that producing fun products often doesn't result in learning. Tell them you want to teach them skills and knowledge that they will actually use after high school, in college or at a job.

The stance I'm taking in this chapter may seem a little confusing. I know that in earlier chapters, I have said that school is a game, and that students must know the rules and play to win. But don't misunderstand me. I'm not saying students should learn, "Milk the system's quirks, and you'll get the results that you want, and everything will be fine." Rather, I'm saying we should teach them, "Know the system's quirks so they won't defeat you, but don't forget that you must also advance personally by mastering new skills and knowledge."

I have also said in earlier chapters that teachers must be likable. Yet in this chapter, I'm saying fun is overrated. Am I contradicting myself? Not really. Being likable doesn't mean entertaining your students instead of teaching them, pandering to their preferences, or shielding them from the real world. It is possible to be both a likable teacher and a teacher who actually educates.

In Defense of the Lecture

My students—the high achievers, the low achievers, and everyone in between—beg me to lecture. I know that is hard to believe, but it's true.

> The studies and commentaries devaluing the lecture are misguided. I think there is more to the story. Lectures can be powerful.

Well . . . it's almost true. They don't exactly beg me. But they do love my lectures. Every year without fail, I get feedback from students saying that they would like me to lecture more. Why? Because with a good lecture, you can shovel out a lot of information in a short period of time. To write a four-page essay on any subject, students need a lot of information.

The lecture has taken a beating in educational studies and commentaries by experts in the field. Many studies point out that kids learn very little from the lecture. The percentage of students said to benefit from lectures is sometimes in the single digits. In other words, we teachers are hearing that if we lecture, we are probably reaching less than 10 percent of our students. Do you remember when milk was good? Well, now it's bad. Eggs once caused increased cholesterol, but now they contain good cholesterol. Butter used to be really bad, but now it is a good option for cooking. Nutrition experts change their minds a lot. The experts in education change their minds even more often. Moreover, the field of education is a far less exact study than nutrition is. If you just wait, the time-tested teaching method of lecturing will come back in vogue.

I think the studies and commentaries devaluing the lecture are misguided. I think there is more to the story. Lectures can be powerful. Think about people considered to be great teachers or leaders, such as Martin Luther King Jr. or Aung San Suu Kyi. Did they lecture? They certainly did, and they successfully changed listeners' thoughts and hearts.

We may never reach these lecturers' skill levels, but we can still become effective speakers. It all comes down to how well we can hold an audience. To keep our students' attention and engage their brains, we need to ask questions—rhetorical questions, viewpoint questions, and leading questions. Please don't dismiss this advice because you feel that you are not a gifted public speaker. You can hold an audience by being yourself. And remember that a good lecture is a good conversation, not a good speech. Play a line or two from a song as an introduction to your lecture. Start with a political cartoon and show students how interesting it really is. Get some props to perk up your lectures. Kids love this approach.

I sometimes feel a little guilty when I lecture, because I'm well aware of the criticism heaped upon the lecture. But then I remind myself that the studies don't explain everything. I know the look of learning on a student's face. I recognize enthusiasm when I see it. Some things just can't be measured by scientific studies. What I know for certain is that when I lecture on my subject matter, my students remember it. They must be listening.

Now, I will concede that there are some good reasons not to over-lecture. For example, school-age kids' brains are developmentally less mature than those of adults. Kids' brains are less able to regulate behavioral impulses. Therefore, be keenly aware of your students' body language. To accommodate the signs you are reading, adjust the length of your lecture and vary pace and volume. You can adjust the number of facts and details without watering down the content. But there's no need to throw out lectures entirely. Check for understanding by using Think-Pair-Share, exit tickets, pointed questions, summaries, and quick writes.

Even if you're skeptical of lectures, or you don't think you can lecture well, consider this: College professors teach by lecture. Employers teach by lecture. Parents teach by lecture. Peers teach by lecture. For example, at the end of a lecture we often hear kids restating the teacher's lecture in the vernacular, with all its modern expressions and idioms. When they put concepts into their own words, they usually retain the lesson. A lecture encourages such exchanges, because students want to validate their understanding of what they just heard. If professors, employers, parents, and peers teach by lecture, shouldn't teachers also teach by lecture? The latest study may not say so, but I urge you to think inside the podium anyway. Please develop your speaking skills. It is worth the effort.

ACTION PLAN

1. Make your lessons more about gaining and demonstrating knowledge and skill and less about producing products.

2. Don't water down your lessons just to make them more fun or so that your students can all pass. In time your students will adjust to a higher standard. Boost their egos with encouragement and sincere praise, but make the work and the test real. Spell out in clear detail what you expect students to be able to *do* at the end of the lesson.

3. Routinely check for understanding in multiple ways.

4. Lecture more if you can pull it off. Don't overdo it, but *do* do it!

CHAPTER 12

Common Core State Standards

At the time of this book's publication, Common Core State Standards (CCSS) are the focus of attention for everyone in the field of education. The current state adoption rate is quite high, but adoption is in a state of flux. Despite the shifts in adoption and the ups and downs in public opinion, it is unlikely that the Common Core movement will diminish.

Trying to figure out the scope and predict the future of any trend in education is like trying to drink water from a fire hydrant. The sheer volume of information will knock you over. To cope with all this information and uncertainty, I think it is productive for teachers to remember that all educational trends contain some truth and some good suggestions, and that these ideas tend to survive no matter what comes next. Without a positive mindset like this, the constant swing of the pendulum could kill our spirits.

Document-Based Questions

What will survive from Common Core? I think a pillar of the movement, the use of document-based questions (DBQs), is one good bet. The world of gifted education has long used DBQs in various forms. Moreover, the AP and IB programs have both used document-based essays for decades.

Let me describe three lessons that use DBQs to help you comply with Common Core standards regardless of the subject matter you teach. These lesson plans are excellent tools for helping your students learn content, practice critical thinking, and hone research skills. The activities in these lessons build in students the qualities that colleges and employers are both looking for.

Lesson One: Analyzing Primary Source Documents (Unwrapping Common Core)

Step One

Begin by collecting primary source documents on the topic you want to teach. These documents can be quotes, political cartoons, photos, letters, and more. The Web is full of such documents. To find them, just use search terms such as *primary source documents Civil War*, *primary source documents English poetry*, or *primary source documents theory of evolution*. Your documents should be about one-fourth to one-half page in length. You'll need eight to twelve documents. Label the documents in a way that will help you and your students distinguish them and keep them organized, such as "Doc A," "Doc B," and so on.

A NOTE ABOUT MATH DBQS

Yes, you can use these lessons for math, too. If you teach math, you might have to make some adjustments to the following instructions. The adjustments are largely a matter of semantics. The key is to think of DBQs as math practice problems. For example, if you are a math teacher, instead of assembling a series of documents that require analytical interpretation, it might be best to create a series of practice problems related to your current unit. To find math problems on the Web, use search terms such as *math problems algebra one*. Label these problems as documents in the same way that other teachers would label their documents.

Each practice problem is a document that adds additional steps for solving. So Document B is a slightly more difficult problem than Document A. As a group, have your students discuss in what ways the documents get progressively more challenging. For example, "What extra step did Document B require to solve the equation that was not present in Document A?" I was a math teacher for ten years, so I know that group discussions that break down the steps to solving problems are invaluable. When a student says during a math lesson, "I don't get it," what the student really means is, "I got lost moving from step three to step four."

Step Two

Type the following questions at the end of each document, in whatever order you prefer. These questions will encourage higher-level thinking and will give you a template for creating great discussion and analysis activities.

- What does the source of this document tell us about the author's viewpoint?

- What are the important details that you see in the document? Why are these details important?

- What is the mood of the document?

- What is the main point of the document? What other perspectives oppose this main point?

- How does this document connect with the subject we are discussing in class? Give examples.

- What previous knowledge would someone need in order to understand the message of this document?

- What would happen if the action this document is suggesting were to be carried out? Or: Predict the responses, both positive and negative, readers might have to the message of this document.

Step Three

Compile the primary source documents, complete with questions, into one handout. Make copies of the handout for all your students. Arrange the students' seats in Socratic Seminar format (a circle and, if necessary, an inner circle). Use the handout to launch a discussion on how to interpret data. This is the essence of Common Core, and it's just the sort of thing many principals love to see underway upon walking into your room.

Lesson Two: Working with Primary Source Documents (Implementing Common Core)

Step One

Now that you have completed a group discussion analyzing the documents, it is time to have students use the documents to answer an essay prompt. For example, let's say you are using primary source documents from the U.S. Civil War period. Here's one possible prompt: "In what ways did Abraham Lincoln change his views on the issue of slavery, based on these documents and your knowledge of U.S. history from 1858 to 1865? Write a three- to four-page response. Use all the documents in your response."

You might protest, "Okay, now you have gone too far. My middle school kids have not developed the abstract thinking skills to accomplish this task!" You may be partly correct, but I encourage you to try this activity anyway. Your students can at least attempt it. So what if their answers are not as sophisticated as those of a senior IB student? The skills they develop will be worth the effort.

> *Have your students write the essay in groups. This is a more fun and less intimidating way to begin. It will serve as a confidence builder for students who struggle with writing and critical thinking.*

Step Two

Have your students write the essay in groups. This is a more fun and less intimidating way to begin. It will serve as a confidence builder for students who struggle with writing and critical thinking. Just make sure that each student turns in his or her own version of the essay. That will prevent individual students from sitting quietly and fading into the woodwork as others put their ideas on paper.

Step Three

Before you read the essays, have students complete an extensive student edit. Reread Chapter 2 to refresh your memory on the details of the peer edit. The student edit not only saves you a lot of time, it is absolutely essential to advancing students' essay writing and analytical thinking skills. The student edit is a strategy that makes it feasible for teachers to assign Common Core activities. I think it is a key teacher survival tactic.

Lesson Three: Using Primary Source Documents to Advance Student Skills (Applying Common Core)

Step One

For this lesson, you'll need a document camera or some other means of projecting your students' work onto a screen. Choose the best example of all the students' essays, a mid-range essay, and a low-range essay. Get permission from the students to use their work, and delete their names from the essays. Share the three essays with your whole class, pointing out what makes the essay good and what weakens it. Try to find both strengths and weaknesses in all three essays. This constructive critique is very important. Do not skip this step, because it is only by seeing real examples that many students realize what they must do to comply with the Common Core standard of writing and analyzing.

And if you skip this step, you'll miss the amazing opportunity to see the lightbulbs of understanding click on during the discussion. Many students hate to write, but when they see how it is actually done—wow, their attitudes change!

> It is only by seeing real examples that many students realize what they must do to comply with the Common Core standard of writing and analyzing.

Step Two

Have the students rewrite their essays. I personally do not read these rewrites. Instead, I make my students get three signatures from their peers verifying that the essay is improved from the original. Once a student has three such signatures, I reward the student by adding a couple of points to the original grade. Remember that a lot of learning happens when students see other students' writing and get ideas about their own writing. That's why it is essential that students get as much feedback as possible on their creative work. This feedback also validates their efforts and motivates students to do well, because they know that their peers will see their work. (And by the way, did you notice that this step creates no extra grading work for you?)

ACTION PLAN

1. Start collecting interesting primary source material, such as quotes, political cartoons, photos, and math problems, from the Internet or from your textbook.

2. Model the analytical process that you expect the group to engage in.

3. Share samples of finished products so that your students will know exactly what you expect of them.

CHAPTER 13

Avoiding Teacher Burnout

When teachers get together and start talking about the teaching profession, what do we often complain about? The list is long, but the items of frustration all fall into two categories: factors outside the realm of our control and factors within the realm of our control. Both of these categories contribute to teacher burnout—when we either try to change things we can't change or neglect what we *can* fix.

Things We Can't Control

I am a good example of the former. After my first three years of teaching, I was completely exhausted. I needed to try something less stressful, so I left education for four years. What happened to me happens to many educators. You see, I expended too much energy and time trying to understand and change realities that were completely beyond my control.

For example, it took me a year to realize that calling parents on the phone may be a blessing or a curse. It's a blessing if the parents work with you. But way too often it's a curse, because many parents are hoping you will just handle the problem without them. Your call has brought them extra work, and they are exhausted. They might find it easier to blame you for the problem instead of their child. They have to live with the child—and you they know only from a distance. News of your phone call may get back to administration, and that could be a double curse.

It took me two hard years to comprehend that behavior referrals don't modify student behavior; they kill a teacher's reputation. Three years elapsed before I realized that middle school kids are in the twilight zone between playful and unpredictable. It also took me that long to realize I was on my own in my classroom and that many administrators would sacrifice a great deal to patch a problem in a politically correct or logistically expedient way.

The fast-swinging pendulum of pedagogy is another common frustration that's outside teachers' control. The current flavor of the year may be differentiated learning; next year it might be backward planning. In the years to follow it might be Common Core, Common Planning, and Common Assessment—culminating in Common Frustration instead of Common Sense. Fast-forward five or ten years, and we'll find another flavor on the ice cream truck. Don't get me wrong: I am not indicting any of these strategies. On the contrary, I believe in the validity of the research supporting them as well

> We teachers often express the opinion that most decision makers outside the classroom have no idea what we face on a daily basis. And we are correct.

as the logic behind their implementation. But let's face it: the swift and constant change complicates an already difficult job.

And it doesn't help that new strategies are often implemented in tricky ways in order to get teachers' buy-in. Administrators might say, "We want your opinion on this," and the next thing you know, the new strategy is established—even if many instructors rejected it. A few years later, that same strategy is abandoned for another new idea. The turnover leaves in its wake the carnage of throngs of educators who have moved on to other professions.

Here are some more realities we can't change. There's nothing we can do about the fact that politicians allow forty students per class in some states, and that some districts don't balance the numbers until three months after school starts. (One year I had seventy students in my third period class until November. They sat on the floor and stood along the walls. They were stuffed into a classroom built for thirty. Why did the administration do that to me and several other teachers? Because legally, they could.) We also can't change the fact that many parents either cannot or do not provide the proper environment for students to study. We can't alter the reality that many ninth graders read at a fifth-grade level. Nor can we change the fact that many students babysit their siblings from

3:00 to 9:00 p.m. All these factors contribute to a feeling of being over-whelmed and a sense of futility.

The realities I've just outlined merely scratch the surface of the prob-lem. They are just a few of the many reasons why educators leave teaching after the first two years. We teachers often express the opinion that most decision makers outside the classroom have no idea what we face on a daily basis. And we are correct.

A Positive View

But we don't need to let all this defeat us. I believe a teacher can find a niche in even the worst educational circumstances. This may sound simple and cliché, but when I close the door to my classroom each morning, I shut out all the negativity I've just described and refocus my energies. It is a constant fight to do this, but it's worth the effort, because my only other option is failure. Following are some strategies I've learned for letting go of the stuff teachers can't change and focusing on what we *can* do. If you disagree with my approach or find it extreme, at least consider how the underlying principles might help you avoid teacher burnout.

Know your limits. Don't try to remember or implement every aspect of every new suggestion that comes down the pike. Pick one new strategy per semester and free your mind of clutter.

> *Staying cool under fire—at least on the outside—will earn you allies in the long run.*

Choose your battles. If the problem that you are trying to deal with is societal in nature, let it go. Be content to change just your little corner of the world.

Try to laugh instead of complain. Teacher gripe sessions contribute to burnout if you take them too seriously or engage in them too often. Take the time to laugh about the futility a little bit.

Don't expect much from administrators, because they are facing a slew of problems similar to yours, and they must deal with a lot of polit-ical issues as well. If your school's administration gives you something, be grateful. Your mission is to learn to survive on your own. Remember that student behavior referrals don't work, and complaining too much will sink your ship.

Don't expect much from parents, either. Unrealistic expectations will leave you frustrated and ready to quit. Speak to parents as often as you can, but remember that they may not share your sense of urgency or your priorities. Or they may simply be unable to do what you would like them to do.

Maintain a positive demeanor. Control all public displays of frustration. People can misinterpret the meaning behind your emotions, and such misunderstandings can make your life miserable. Staying cool under fire—at least on the outside—will earn you allies in the long run.

ACTION PLAN

1. Close the door to your classroom in the morning and focus only on your students and your teaching. Keep all other issues outside the walls of the classroom. Your students will notice and follow your example, and all of you will be slower to blow a fuse.

2. Remember that most of your students aren't mature, logical, or experienced. Expect irrational behavior. Don't let it get you down. Parents may provide little or no relief. Move on quickly to the items that you can change. That is how you find joy and endure in this profession.

3. Administrators want low-maintenance teachers. It is in your best interest to play that role. Remember that their hands, like yours, are tied. Complaining about something that can't be fixed is a waste of time and makes enemies out of friends.

4. Never give student behavior referrals without seriously counting the cost. There is a great risk involved to your reputation. It is usually not worth it.

PART I SUMMARY

Some teachers, after twenty or more years in the profession, still take work home every night and log sixty hours a week at school. Are they better teachers than those who rarely take work home? Perhaps, but it's not because of the hours they put in. In fact, I would argue that they may lack balance and organization, and therefore, they may actually weigh in at the light end of the scale that measures good teaching.

In the preceding chapters, I have proposed that teachers must let go of the paperwork and refocus on the person. I've offered examples of how to teach without carrying the heavy burden of clerical work, without bleeding your energy dry with rivers of red ink, and without endlessly recording plagiarized products. I've argued that much of what we record doesn't need recording, that much of what students produce doesn't need producing, and that much of what both teachers and students do simply doesn't need to be done.

> Some teachers, after twenty or more years in the profession, still take work home every night and log sixty hours a week at school. Are they better teachers than those who rarely take work home? Perhaps, but I would argue that they may lack balance and organization.

I hope I have been persuasive. I hope that you will choose to offer your personality, humor, and insight to your students rather than trudging along the paper trail of the modern U.S. education system. I hope I have convinced you that work does not necessarily equal ability, knowledge, or wisdom. It's the quality of work—the teacher's and the students'—that makes the difference.

Consider that for much of the day, twenty-first-century students avoid direct interaction with humans in favor of texting and social media. Consider also how much general daily activity, from shopping to banking to scheduling appointments, takes place online. I wonder when schools will all be online? It may happen sooner than we think. How do we as teachers fit into this equation? Are we encouraging students to disconnect from people and plug into devices? Or are we encouraging them to unplug and interact? If our assignments are largely work-driven and product-producing, we are driving students apart. If our assignments are driven by human interaction, we are bringing them together. The latter brings greater rewards for both the student and the teacher, and it requires less work for the teacher.

When a teacher has a total of more than 200 students, as I do, teaching and grading the traditional way generates a blizzard of paperwork. The volume is unimaginable to a layperson. When I hear so-called "experts" in education propose solutions that have no basis in reality, I get pretty angry. Their plans and ideas usually assume that a class has twenty-five to thirty students who are all at the same level. But many modern classrooms have thirty-five to forty students at varying levels. These numbers do not adhere to theory, do not succumb to emotion, and do not subscribe to a political party— they simply tell us that modern middle schools and high schools are far more challenging places to teach and to learn than many experts think. Whatever they ask of teachers, it is safe to assume that they have underestimated the workload considerably.

> If our assignments are largely work-driven and product-producing, we are driving students apart. If our assignments are driven by human interaction, we are bringing them together. The latter brings greater rewards for both the student and the teacher, and it requires less work for the teacher.

Something has to give. I think paperwork should be the first thing to go. Do whatever you can on your end to avoid creating unnecessary paperwork for yourself. Give fewer assignments that need to be graded by you—the key word here is *you*. Carefully reread Chapters 2 and 3 on using TAs, student helpers, and the peer editing process. Even if you disagree with some of the points made in these chapters, let the information trigger your creative thinking.

If you're still unsure about the approach I'm suggesting, I offer you one more story to consider before we move on to Part 2. I remember vividly a teacher at my school who read every single essay her students wrote and used her red pen to make glorious marks from top to bottom. The copious, complex red commentary looked like the system of arteries, veins, and capillaries in the human body. It was marvelous and meticulous in its scope and detail. I encountered a student who held one of these impressively marked essays with a bright red grade of 62 percent written in the top right corner of the page. I asked the student what he thought of the comments in the margins, at the beginning, at the end, and in the wonderful attachment the teacher had stapled to the essay. "How does this feedback help you?" I asked. "Not at all," the student muttered. "I haven't read the comments." "Why?" I asked. "I don't care what she thinks. I just can't believe she gave me a sixty-two. I spent two hours on this! I hate her!" And so it goes in the mind of the average sixteen-year-old.

PART 1 ACTION PLAN
Decrease Your Workload and Increase the Payoff

You might want to attach this list to the front cover of your lesson-planning book.

1. **What assignments are worth giving?** Give assignments in which the information and work done will appear in future tests. If you do this, students will know that you will hold them accountable for learning and not just producing. Chapter 1 has a specific list of good versus bad assignments.

2. **How do you accurately grade forty essays in forty minutes?** Start by using the peer edit to prepare the essays for your reading. Next, keep the principles of the rubric in your head. Do not worry about marking the essay with a red pen. With practice comes speed. There is more to this skill, though. Chapter 2 offers specific techniques.

3. **What can your TA do for you?** Most of your paperwork. Test this out using the advice in Chapter 3, and you will find great joy. You will also improve as an educator.

4. **How can you be likable as a teacher?** Chapter 4 examines several ways to be likable. Remember: if students believe that you like them and that you have their best interests at heart, you will be liked regardless of your personality.

5. **Have you tried the Socratic Seminar?** If not, now is the time. You will create buy-in and a love for your class among students. Students work harder for teachers they love. Reread Chapter 5 to refresh your memory on conducting Socratic Seminars.

6. **What can AVID do for you?** Build a team. Strengthen student accountability. Help you reteach and cement concepts. These three reasons are just a start. For more, take another peek at Chapter 6.

7. **Is there a better way to grade homework?** Yes! Don't grade it at all. Have students grade it in class or have a TA or student helper

→

complete the task for you. Use the pass/fail system. Teach more; grade less. This strategy produces better results, as Chapter 7 shows.

8. **What exactly do you teach?** You teach a great deal more than just the subject matter, I hope. To maximize learning, you must know your students, and they must know you. The Boulder Creek philosophy explained in Chapter 8 shows the way.

9. **What are your classroom rules?** Some rules work better than others. Chapter 9 explains how to make student behavior a one-on-one challenge instead of a forty-against-one battle.

10. **How can you use lesson plans to pair good grades with a love of learning?** By creating lessons that not only have clearly defined objectives, but also employ the power of competition. Competition can motivate when other strategies fail, as you saw in Chapter 10.

11. **Are you keeping your students busy making products?** The fact that a student has completed an assignment does not necessarily mean that the student has mastered the objective. Products do not equal knowledge. Chapter 11 points out that you have to continue to examine why you are giving out work.

12. **Are you ready for Common Core State Standards?** Common Core is not only the flavor of the day, but it also has some valid strategies and objectives. Chapter 12 gives some practical lesson plans to help you comply.

13. **How close to burnout are you?** I have been there and back! To avoid burnout, manage your workload. Manage how you are perceived by administrators and parents. Manage your complaining about things that are out of your control. You'll find plenty more advice in Chapter 13.

PART 2

Teach Your Students the Path to Higher Grades

I suggest that you read aloud key portions of this part of the book during advisory or homeroom class or as a warm-up activity, and follow up the reading with a brief discussion. I have written this section with this purpose in mind. Relevant passages speak to the student as well as the teacher.

CHAPTER 14

So Your Students Don't Like to Read

A few years ago at Cajon High School in San Bernardino, we had some "average" students who scored really well on the SAT. Their scores were significantly higher than any we had seen before. One student was a young lady who was homeless, sometimes living in a van. After she received invitations from several elite universities, we asked her to explain how she scored so well on the SAT. She said that she'd learned to escape the hell of her environment by reading novels and magazines. She thought that all the reading she'd done in the van probably made a big difference. This revelation made a big impact on me and Mr. Peters, our school's AVID coordinator, but it didn't really impress anyone else—especially the other students.

I keep trying to convince young people how important reading is to academic achievement, to job success, to life relationships, to almost everything that can be done—but it's a tough sell. The movie stars, musicians, athletes, and politicians on the posters in our school library haven't had much luck, either. Even our school's homeless SAT champ failed to get her peers' attention. Though I haven't convinced all my students to develop a love for reading, I have found some strategies for winning over some students.

The Sworn Statement

One year I came up with an idea to motivate students to read. I thought that since many students would rather poke themselves in the eye than read a textbook, I could offer extra credit for reading. I simply gave a reading assignment of about seven pages—not so long that it was discouraging, not so short that it was a joke. How could I hold them accountable? Give a quiz the next day? They protested with the force of a Category 5 hurricane. Okay, how about a sworn statement with a signature?

That sounds crazy, doesn't it? If you have read this book up to this point, you have surely noticed my lack of trust in the honesty of the average teenager. But I figured I had nothing to lose. No other strategy had ever worked for me or any other educator with whom I had discussed this problem. So why not try something crazy for once?

I told my students to be creative and funny with their sworn statements, and that they should swear by something that they personally really believed in—no matter what that something might be. I gave a Jonathan Edwards–style Puritan speech, saying that fire would rain down from heaven and devour them if they lied in their statements. They laughed, but they loved my theatrics. I gently pumped a few foreheads and shouted, "Demons be gone!" to cast out any possible evil influence. They loved that even more.

I was prepared to be shocked by my students' statements. They didn't disappoint me. And you know what? I don't believe they lied—at least most of them. (Perhaps the ones who swore on the soul of Mary Juana lied just a little.) Their sworn statements were creative and funny, as requested. But more importantly, most of the students scored well on the next test. I proved my point that reading makes a difference in student learning and in academic success. It made a difference for a good portion of the year.

This method wasn't perfect, though. The novelty eventually wore off, and my students went back to their old ways. So remember that the sworn statement is by no means a permanent solution. Nevertheless, this tactic started a love for reading for several students. In addition, although the effect was only temporary, it lasted long enough to change students' mindsets about reading in general. Hopefully, this adjustment in viewpoint opened the door to a future love of reading. Sometimes that is as good as it gets for educators. We change their thinking just a little, and a future teacher can change their actions a lot. And there is nothing wrong with that!

Assignment with Quick Write and Sworn Statement

Here is a step-by-step guide to the process that worked for me. Why not give it a try?

1. Assign about seven pages of reading. If the material is any longer, students may not read it. If it's any shorter, it's not worth the effort.

2. Tell your students that when they finish the reading, they should turn the book facedown and begin a quick write. Explain that a quick write means writing one page of whatever comes to mind in whatever order, without worrying about spelling or grammar. Remind students that they must not look at the book while they write; their writing must come from their head only. The point here is that if the reading is to be useful, it must be remembered. No copying is allowed. If students can write only a couple of sentences (or less), then they may stop writing and reread the material. After the reread, they must put the book facedown and begin writing again where they left off. This method will soon train a student's brain to remember what it reads. That's because it takes less work to remember than it does to read a text over and over again. In this way, your students will be able to use the information from the reading to complete a test or an essay. Why? Because now they have that information stored in their brains, and they can retrieve it for use when they need it.

3. Have your students turn in their one-page quick writes to you. (Yes, they do this quick write at home, and no, they will not all cheat.) At the end of this page, instruct them to write a sworn statement. Here's a real-life example: "I, Tom Jones III, swear on the love of my favorite video game and my mother's love and support that I, Tom Jones III, have read pages 123 to 129 and did not copy my quick write but wrote every word from my huge head. Signed, Tom Jones III." (I have received many statements that were far funnier than this one, but they weren't fit to print.)

The Importance of Reading

Do whatever you can to convince the young people in your care that developing a love for reading can translate into academic success and less work in the long run. They may not believe you, but if you can connect reading assignments to the final grade students receive in your class, then perhaps they will pay attention and read nonetheless. (The Action Plan for this chapter gives two easy ways to connect reading to the grade.) When all else fails, most students still want to pass your class. They don't really want to see you again next year.

There's another good reason to make reading assignments part of your classroom curriculum: it's simply a good teaching practice. Once upon a time, my students loved me for lecturing *everything*. I spoon-fed them every possible fact or test question. I would say proudly that if I hadn't said something out loud, then it would not appear on the test. I always kept my word. But eventually I stopped using this method. I found that I could say only so much in class, and relying so heavily on lectures favored the auditory learners to an unfair extent. Moreover, I realized that I was not preparing my students adequately for jobs or college; in both of these, reading retention is key to success.

ACTION PLAN

1. Give your students extra-credit reading assignments. You can control grade inflation by the number of points you assign. Remember: getting students engaged in reading is good for everyone.

2. Assign a short reading passage with a quick write and a sworn statement every day. This will not add work to your busy day, because it involves no grading. Students either write the quick write and receive full credit or they don't write it and receive a zero.

3. Discuss the following questions with your students:

   • What is your attitude toward reading? Why?

   • What parts of this chapter do you agree or disagree with?

   • How important is it to academic success to learn to like or love reading? Why?

   • What lessons can you take away from this chapter?

CHAPTER 15

Teach Your Students How to Be Organized

A student accused me of failing to record an assignment that he'd done. (I suspect every teacher has this experience virtually every day.) I replied, "Well, you're probably right. Show me the assignment in your notebook." The student's notebook was so disorganized that after several minutes of frustrated searching, he gave up his quest. In my experience, this type of disorganization is the norm, not the exception. And this little story highlights a handy truth: It takes less work to be organized than it does to solve the problems caused by being disorganized.

The Value of Organization

I've noticed that many students are eager to discard work almost immediately after it is returned to them. It seems as if keeping this work is a painful reminder of how they sacrificed part of their lives to complete this assignment. Perhaps people just have a natural tendency to move on after a task is completed. Whatever the reason for student disorganization, the effect is often the same. Better organization predicts better success in most academic endeavors, and disorganization predicts less success. So when it comes to coursework of any kind, teach your students to keep their work until the final grade has been posted on their transcripts.

But why do you have to teach your students to stay organized? Perhaps you are thinking that this is not your job and that you have more important things to do. You're probably right. But if you are interested in making a real difference in the lives of your students, then your ideas about the scope of your job must transcend traditional thought. Just like the knowledge and skills you teach, organization is key to operating effectively in society. Organization not only makes work easier, it also makes that work more attractive and understandable to others.

I think this principle applies almost universally. I remember being persuaded to buy one used car over another based on the neatness of the service records. I remember hiring one realtor over another based on her neat notebook of listings. I remember purchasing one television brand instead of another because the former's box sported an organized explanation of its functions. The examples could go on and on.

The rule applies to students, too. The smallest things can make a big impression. For example, consider a student who tabulates her three-ring binder and a student who stuffs papers in willy-nilly. Which student looks better to you? A well-organized binder makes a strong impression on a teacher. To a teacher, a tidy student notebook is like catnip to a cat.

Getting Organized: Tips for Students

Following are several ideas for teaching your students to work, study, and keep records in an organized way. I have written this section to address students, so you can read aloud or otherwise share this material directly with your class.

Prioritize Your Homework

Choose the order of assignments you do each night by their possible effects on your final grades for those classes. For example, studying for a biology test would be more important than doing a history crossword puzzle. Don't prioritize your work by how much you enjoy it or by the sequence of your school day (period one, period two, and so on).

Make Flash Cards

Over the years, I have interviewed thousands of students to find out how they get organized to study for a test. The number one response from students who performed well is making flash cards. This makes absolute sense if you think about it. While you create the cards, you are learning, organizing, and reviewing the information. If you later have someone test you using the cards, you are cementing the information while doing something fun with a friend.

Avoid Cramming for Tests

Yes, everyone crams. But that doesn't mean it's a good idea. It actually takes less effort and brings better results to be organized and do a little studying each day. Maybe you think, "Well, if I do a little each day, then I will forget by the time the test comes. It's better to study all at once right before the test, because I will have a better chance of remembering the information." It's not true. Although educators rarely agree on any subject, they almost universally agree that cramming is a poor studying strategy. If you find this hard to believe, research this topic. Or just once, try studying little by little and see what happens.

Pick a Partner or Form a Study Group

Studying with a partner or study group can help you get organized and learn more effectively. If you are not an organized person by nature, working with someone else may help you. You will be able to see how another person's mind categorizes ideas. And when you study with others, you engage more of your senses. Seeing and hearing and talking about material is more effective than studying alone, without sound or movement. A few laughs, a few mistakes, and a few facial expressions added to your study will boost both fun and retention. You'll remember more information, and you'll dread the work less. This strategy is great practice for college, too. If your circumstances do not allow you to leave home for group study, use this strategy via phone or webcam.

> *Organization not only makes work easier, it also makes that work more attractive and understandable to others.*

Save Your Work Carefully

Organize your completed work by subject and then by date. You could also organize it by topic, but sometimes the wording of topics can cause confusion. Finding an assignment by a date is usually easier than finding an assignment by a topic. Also, most teachers enter work with dates as well as titles, so chronological order is your best bet.

ACTION PLAN

1. Please, teach your students how to be organized. You may be the only teacher in their entire education to help them learn this key life lesson.

2. Use the material in this chapter for a Socratic Seminar. Or if you prefer, read and discuss the key points with your students. They may offer some great tips not mentioned here—tips that everyone, including you, can use.

3. Have your students share with the class the worst organizational disasters that have happened to them or someone they know. This will get them thinking about the need to change.

4. Give this optional student assignment: Written reflection (two pages): "Students with good organizational skills are more successful in school and in life." To what extent do you agree with this statement?

CHAPTER 16

How to Improve Students' Attitudes

Empathy is a powerful changer of hearts. Responsibility is more productive than blame. Respect makes school easier for everyone. To create an environment that fosters learning instead of hampering it, encourage students to develop an attitude of empathy, responsibility, and respect.

From Dislike to Empathy

For adults, it is hard to remember the strong emotions adolescents feel. These emotions can be so strong that they overwhelm common sense or even a student's own self-interest. For example, many students will not perform in a classroom setting for one reason: they simply don't like the teacher or the people in the class. I'm constantly amazed at how young people transfer their feelings about one situation or person to an unrelated situation or person and act accordingly.

For example, Jonathan will not do Ms. Garcia's homework because Ms. Garcia likes Henry, and Henry is an enemy. Saundra will not complete her group assignment, because Jane is in her group, and Jane told Jonathan about Saundra's feelings for him. Well, Jane will pay when Saundra turns in her section of the assignment. Let's see how she likes that!

You certainly can't mediate all your students' social conflicts. But you can help them know one another better and develop empathy. Empathy works wonders on student attitudes. Following is an example of this phenomenon from my own classroom.

My elective class began with student readings of their personal statements. When I assign these statements, I give students the following prompt: "Tell us what we are missing by looking only at the written records of your school career, such as your GPA or transcript. What are your story and your attitude about school?" I have my students read aloud their responses to this prompt in front of the class. Afterward, students who are listening must give feedback that will help improve the essay.

On one particular day, a student whom we will call Paul read his personal statement. Few people in class (including me) knew anything at all about Paul. I thought he was probably an average or below-average student, because he rarely spoke. Then we heard the following story.

> When students share their personal struggles and find that they have some common traits, then the classroom transforms. It feels more like a family than just an academic holding tank for strangers.

Paul's Story

When I was seven years old, I was legally separated from both my mother and father because of so many domestic violence calls the police had to come to our house and deal with. My father was always drunk and violent when the police came. A social worker would often come to our house and investigate the situation.

We lived in a two-room house with bad sanitation, little clothing, and not enough food for everybody to eat. We relied on food stamps as our income. Beer bottles were lying around everywhere.

The social worker felt that I was in danger in my own house. As the years passed, I moved from foster home to foster home seven times. When I finally got adopted by my grandmother, I felt real joyful, because I could now be living with somebody that was part of my family.

I moved in with her when I was ten years old, and for two years, everything was going great and I was a very happy child. Then all of a sudden my grandma did not have the same love for me as she used to. I saw her change rapidly, which made me feel very lonely at times and made me cry as well.

My grandma has changed a lot ever since I started getting into my teenage years. She calls me insulting names relating to my father and talks about how I have the same characteristics as he does and how I will become the way he is when I am older. At times she locks me out of my own house and makes me stay out there for a couple of hours in the cold just because she does not want to glimpse me because I remind her of my dad.

At my grandma's house, I do my own laundry, cook my own food, and do household chores. In my spare time I leave the house and wander the streets to get my mind off the horrid experiences I've had. Even wandering the streets is a negative thing to do, because there are more problems out there than there are in my house. So sometimes it is hard to make a decision whether I should leave or stay in my house.

I consider myself a hardworking, determined, and successful student at school. Surprisingly, all these things that I have mentioned above and all this negative feedback from my grandma have not affected my education. I am determined for it not to happen.

After four or five students gave Paul feedback, the entire group dynamic changed for the better. The students not only felt empathy toward Paul but also displayed more respect and thoughtfulness in general.

Why? Well, you see, students had been heard. And that means so much to young adults. When students share their personal struggles and find that they have some common traits, then the classroom transforms. It feels more like a family than just an academic holding tank for strangers.

In other words, attitudes change. Attitudes become kinder, more tolerant, and more respectful. Words become more supportive, helpful, and insightful. Thinking becomes more positive and more analytical. Grades begin to rise as a result of all these improvements.

Here's what happened in Ms. Garcia's class after all the students read aloud their statements. Jonathan realized that Henry is struggling with Asperger's. Jonathan had been tempted to bully Henry. He realized that was cruel. Henry has a serious problem. Jonathan resolved to defend Henry. He realized Henry has overcome a lot and is cool to have made it that far.

When Saundra listened to Jane's personal statement, she learned that Jane has a brother with special needs who is always the focus of everyone in the family. Jane never gets to talk about what is happening in her life. It's always about her brother. Saundra felt different about Jane after learning this. She figured out why Jane talks about other people so much. She resolved not to take offense at Jane's gossip and no longer wanted to hurt Jane by sabotaging the group project.

From Blame to Responsibility

Why do kids try to shift the blame for their problems? For the same reasons we do. Sometimes we are just not ready to face or change reality. This avoidance is counterproductive, and as educators we should redirect attitudes. Make it your classroom culture to promote positive attitudes and ban negative ones.

Kids can be especially quick to blame the teacher. What attitudes should teachers prohibit students from displaying in their classrooms?

1. It is your fault because you did not teach this well.

2. You owe me another chance at this.

3. You favor so-and-so.

4. You are boring.

5. You did not talk about this topic in class, so it should not count on the test.

6. You have to postpone the test; we have other classes too, you know.

7. Your TA always messes up my paper.

8. You forgot to grade my work.

9. You must have lost my work, because I know for a fact that I did it.

10. Mr. Ibrahim is a better teacher than you. He never did this to us last year.

What is the common thread in these comments? Blame, of course. Do not allow students to play the blame game in your class. How do you direct this change? A frank group discussion about taking responsibility and avoiding blame is probably the best vehicle.

From Rudeness to Respect

Discuss the following questions and ideas in a Socratic Seminar with your students. I've addressed this section to students, so you can share it with them directly.

What is a good attitude? It is full of humility, overflows with curiosity, spills out honesty, displays kindness. A good attitude is humorous and sincere. It accepts blame, it offers help without hope of profit, it accepts the good with the bad, and it asks for help at the risk of humiliation.

What is a bad attitude? It is a display of negative body language, tone of voice, and demeanor. One bad attitude can make an entire class seem intolerable to everyone. Your attitude is contagious. Have you seen one student change the whole atmosphere of a classroom? How does your teacher see you? Are you a force for good or more like a virus that might infect others?

> *Attitudes become kinder, more tolerant, and more respectful. Words become more supportive, helpful, and insightful. Thinking becomes more positive and more analytical. Grades begin to rise as a result of all these improvements.*

What does your body language usually say? Many of the negative attitudes teachers may direct at you come from reading your body language. For example, if your body is facing your friend during a lecture, then you're sending your teacher the following message: "Hurry up and look the other way or finish yammering so I can get back to talking with my friend."

Is sleeping during a lecture or lesson a good idea? No. Texting? No. Wearing headphones? No. Doing homework? No. Eating? No. Side conversations? No. This list could go on and on. The only respectful way to act during a lecture is to sit quietly and look engaged and interested— even if you're bored to death. It won't kill you. And doing this is good practice for life and work.

ACTION PLAN

1. Please don't be so worried about covering curriculum that you fail to see the student. You will actually cover more topics and objectives when attitudes are in balance. Attitudes must be taught and adjusted by you.

2. Remember that no learning takes place without a relationship. Your job as a teacher is to make relationship building as easy for your students as possible by helping them know one another better.

3. Do not allow an attitude of blame from anyone in your classroom.

4. Remember that attitudes can change. When the attitude of your class becomes negative, conduct a Socratic Seminar to make an attitude adjustment.

5. Discuss the following questions with your students:

   • What is your attitude toward your teacher? Why?

   • What parts of this chapter do you agree or disagree with?

   • How important is it to display the right attitude?

   • What is a good attitude? Why?

   • What lessons can we take away from this chapter?

CHAPTER 17
Avoid Glorifying the D Culture

In my opinion, many American schools sorely lack a culture in which individuals take personal responsibility for their academic performance. This is what I call the D culture. In the D culture, there are many reasons why Sally did not do well—but none of them is Sally's fault or her family's fault or society's fault. The reasons are always your fault, teacher.

I am fascinated at how strong the D culture has grown in recent years. Some young people are no longer ashamed or embarrassed to have a report card sporting a 1.5 GPA. Many accept academic failure as okay—or even something to celebrate with their peers. They often laugh at, joke about, praise, and accept horrific GPAs with no qualms whatsoever. I call this glorifying the D culture.

The Evolution of the D Culture

I have watched this change happen slowly but steadily throughout my teaching career. Here's how the cultural transformation looks to me:

- In 1960 getting a D was shameful.

- In 1970 getting a D was a bummer.

- In 1980 getting a D could happen at times if you weren't careful.

- In 1990 getting a D could happen if you were in a bad school or had a bad teacher.

- In 2000 getting a D was not the student's fault but was the result of misplaced expectations that could be fixed with legislation.

- In 2010 getting a D was okay because you could get it changed through summer school, with an online course, or if your parent complained.

Young people have become more and more accepting of everyone in recent years. That is a good thing, right? It certainly is, in most cases! But unquestioning acceptance is not a good thing when it transforms into glorifying slackers.

Whatever else you may believe, one thing is clear: the stigma and fear of getting a D is not what it once was. Who knows where this transformation will end?

Offer Something Better

The D culture is one of your greatest challenges as a teacher. Many of your students are not motivated to do well in school. They can't see the point. They lack pride in their academic achievements. Some students just prefer to fit in with their D friends. These are the students who embrace the D culture because they believe it is in their best interest socially to do so. Finally, there are students who quit trying because they haven't experienced enough success in the past to keep them going in the present.

Don't ignore this reality. Be no party to the D culture. Offer students something better. Teach them to have pride in themselves, their work, and the ideas they represent.

Perhaps the easiest way is by personal recognition. Express something like the following in your class, in earshot of all: "Hey, I want to take a moment at the start of class to recognize the following five students . . . they have shown outstanding improvement this semester, not missing one single homework assignment." The two minutes that it takes to make this announcement may cause five students—hopefully more—to continue down the path to success. It is worth the time, because it changes the culture of your class.

Here is another very specific strategy for fighting the D culture: Enlist the help of alumni. Have former students, especially ones who were struggling, come back and speak to the class about how they eventually conquered peer pressure and are now successful. Social media is an easy way to find these former students. We do this every year in my class. I am continually amazed by the impact a former student can have on a current student.

Kids need to see proof for the ideas you're selling in a living person from their neighborhood and school. Don't miss out on this opportunity.

I was mesmerized by the stillness in the room when a former student of mine who was an ex–gang member shared with the class how he left his gang and graduated from California Polytechnic State University. He expressed that what helped him most in high school was the fact that one of his teachers, Mr. Peters, continually saw him as a real person with potential. By the time he turned twenty-four and came back to visit my class, he was making six figures as an engineer. When he was finished speaking, he asked, "Are there any questions?" Forty hands went up. You don't see that very often!

This endeavor to offer something better than the D culture is worth the effort, because the effort reflects your values. In addition, our schools are not producing enough skilled workers for a future economy. Skilled workers are people who embrace individual responsibility and strive to do their best. Educators can do something about this. Yes, we already have too much to do—but if we don't address this issue in our classrooms, what difference will it make that we worked hard on everything else?

In a typical urban high school in a low income area, 1,000 freshmen students enter the school each year. Four years later, fewer than 500 of those students leave the school with a diploma. Now some will quibble with these numbers, but we all can see with our own eyes how many students start compared to how many finish. Whatever the exact numbers are, the question remains: why do so many students drop out? I propose that a key reason is peer pressure glorifying the D culture. Students give up largely because they cannot handle the pressures of being teenagers and work on their GPAs at the same time.

To fight back against the D culture, inform your students of these important truths:

- Most of your friends from high school will not remember your name in five years.

- In less than two years, you will not speak to most of your friends from high school.

- If you sacrifice your grades for your friends, they will not remember or care in the short run or in the long run—but you will live with this decision forever.

Once your students understand these realities, you can give them this advice:

- Never be ashamed of doing better than your friends. If they are really your friends, then they will celebrate your success. You'll know they are not true friends and are just using you if they make fun of your efforts toward academic success. By doing so, they feel better about their own failures.

- People often criticize or make fun of people or ideas out of fear, anger, ignorance, or a sense of inferiority. You do not serve your friends by fueling their illogical fears and poor attitudes.

Remember, one of the biggest challenges you'll face in teaching students is the double whammy of your school's academic culture combined with the peer pressure that is prevalent in every school. The secret to success—for both you and your students—is your commitment to rise above what you see in the school system that isn't working.

ACTION PLAN

1. Fight the D culture because this effort will transform how students work in your classroom. It will mean less late work, less copying, less bad attitude, fewer excuses, and less stress for you.

2. Convince students that higher grades are worth both the effort of achieving them and the teasing students might receive.

3. Remind students that gaining the approval of their friends should never mean sacrificing their GPAs.

4. Remind students that they should not be ashamed of doing better academically than their friends. True friends will celebrate one another's successes.

CHAPTER 18

Changing Your Students' Goals

For twenty-five years, I have watched students of all conceivable abilities pigeonhole, stereotype, predestine, and sabotage themselves into a lower grade. They do this simply because of their own preconceptions about who they are academically.

Self-Fulfilling Expectations

Seventeen-year-old Jamal is a good example of this phenomenon. He is excited when he notices on the math class grade printout that he ranks number one in the class. This seems unreal to him. "How can this be?" he thinks. "I am a B student in almost all my classes. Always have been and probably always will be. Oh yeah, there have been times when I got an A, but that teacher was easy," he rationalizes.

Jamal's beliefs about who he is and who he will be academically come from his decade in the school system. After all, fifty-plus teachers have told him, since the moment that he entered first grade, that he is a B student. They may not have walked up to him and said, "Hey, Jamal, you are a B student, so just face it." But he got the message loud and clear from their actions and expectations.

Logic tells Jamal that his current A in math is his teacher's doing, not his own. The fifty teachers who came before this one can't all be wrong. So the likelihood is that Jamal won't stay long at the top. He will fulfill his own expectations about himself.

It has been fascinating to watch so many students, just like Jamal, put forth just the right amount of effort to fulfill their own expectations. I have seen many students with a 99 percent average for the semester go into a final exam convinced that they will fail, because they always get a B for their final grade. And—lo and behold—they do indeed fail the test.

Perhaps this is the choice that, subconsciously, they are most comfortable with. I'm no psychologist, so I won't delve deeply into the psychological reasons behind such behavior. But whatever the reason, I do know that this happens over and over and over and over—every year, with every teacher. The longer a student's academic history is, the harder it is for that student to break free of his or her perceived academic destiny.

Debunking the Idea of Destiny

Teach your students that their grade in your class is not inherited. It is not written in the software—or the stars. You have no fixed idea of who they are academically, and neither should they. The following tips can help your students change their goals and expectations. This list is written to address students, so you can share it with them directly.

- One point over the course of a whole semester can make the mathematical difference between an A and a B final grade. One point here and one point there and another here and another there add up over time.

- One point on one assignment could change your grade.

- One extra comment during a class discussion could give you an extra participation point.

- Spending one second more on a multiple-choice test could help you see the obvious answer and score one point higher.

- Writing one extra sentence on an essay could add one more point to your score.

- Asking one more question after class could earn you the extra-credit point you need to bump your grade up a notch.

- One grumble fewer earns you a six instead of a five on class participation.

- No one is predestined to get or not get certain points. You get points when you work to earn them. You are in control.

- Your academic habits play a large role in your determining grades. You can create or change your own habits. Create good habits by listening, taking notes, and reading with a purpose. You can be kind, be humble, and show self-control.

- Observe and imitate the work habits of A students.

Writing One's Own Story

If your students are having trouble shaking the feeling that they simply are destined to become what past teachers and report cards have told them they are, share the story of Tyra (not her real name) with them. It is part of a personal statement read to my class by one of my students. It illustrates that no matter what others think of us, and no matter what sort of environment we've inherited, we are what *we* make of ourselves. Our attitudes and goals make all the difference.

Tyra's Story

My family loves to party and drink, then get ignorant. I have lived in a box, and this box consists of a wicked family who are not mine. At age four I was separated from my mother and five brothers. As a child, I thought this was the worst that could happen, because I lost the people that I grew up with.

I was sadly mistaken. My life got worse. When I was at my lowest, I got the evil stepmother people only read about. My sister's mother helped raise me—not as a mother should raise a child, but as a monster who had no feelings. She would make me wash all the clothes, do all the dishes, and clean the floor while she sat around and did nothing.

My father never believed me when I told him how she treated me. He believed she was simply following the schedule. My father would tell me that he didn't want me to end up pregnant at age sixteen. He thought she was right to be so strict with me.

I knew I was smarter than this, but I simply agreed and continued with my life. The one person in my family who could provide an escape for me was my uncle Benjamin, also known as Bobo. He was everything to me, and as long as I had him, nothing could go wrong.

At age nine my world was shattered when he was shot, killed, and taken from me without reason. My uncle's death showed me that life is short, and we need to make the most of it while we are alive. Having a wicked stepmother proved to me that with strong willpower and a little time, I can overcome anything.

I will do better than my parents. I will make a name for myself. I don't need a prince like Cinderella did; I can make my own happy ending.

And indeed Tyra did. She graduated high school with a 3.7 GPA and is currently a successful college student. How can you use this in your classroom? Read the story to your students and discuss it with them. Expand the discussion by using point number five of the following Action Plan. Or, if you prefer, use these questions as an assignment for a reflective essay.

ACTION PLAN

Tell your students:

1. Destiny doesn't exist. You, like Tyra, can make your own happy ending. Believe that you are an A student.

2. Observe the habits of the A students in your class—especially those who are not intellectually gifted. What do they do that you don't do? Imitate their habits.

3. Take just a couple of minutes a day to check your grades. Ask yourself, "How could I have gotten a few points more on that last assignment? Remember, a point here and a point there can bring your grade up over time.

4. Never be in a hurry to finish a test. Work from bell to bell. If you are in class for fifty-three minutes, use that time wisely. You will have plenty of time for fun and socializing outside of class.

5. Discuss the following questions:

   • Have your grades been consistent over the years? Why?

   • What parts of this chapter do you agree or disagree with?

   • How important is it to believe that you are an A student? Why?

   • What lessons can you take away from this chapter?

CHAPTER 19

Grade Destroyer Number One: Teacher Grading System Confusion

You can use the information in this chapter as notes for a lecture. Or you could simply have your students read the chapter, then follow up the reading with a class discussion. I've written this chapter to address students directly.

The mathematical method a teacher uses to determine a final grade is a mystery to many secondary students and their parents. Frank is a good example of this problem. Frank is confused, bewildered, surprised, and saddened when Izzy gets a B and he gets a C in their U.S. history class. You see, Frank knows that he did more work than Izzy, that he scored higher on the tests, that he did a better project, and most importantly, that he knows a lot more than she does about U.S. history.

What happened? Simply this: Izzy knew how the computer would figure her grade and which assignments would have the greatest impact. She does not have a higher IQ, a stronger work ethic, a more supportive family, or anything else that could explain her higher grade. However, she understands her teacher's grading formula.

Izzy and Frank's teacher uses a total points grading system. This is one of the two most common grading systems. The other is the weighted grade system. Following are overviews of both.

The Total Points Grading System

Most teachers use a computer program that allows a teacher to assign a point value for each assignment. After your teacher enters all the points you've earned, the computer does the math and spits out a percentage for your final grade. Let's say that in the course of one semester, your teacher enters five graded assignments into the computer:

- Assignment one is a project with 50 possible points.

- Assignment two is a midterm test with 200 possible points.

- Assignment three is a paper with 50 possible points.

- Assignment four is a final exam with 200 possible points.

- Assignment five is attendance and class participation, worth 500 possible points.

Under this grading system, a student could earn one thousand points with perfect work. One thousand points out of one thousand would translate to a grade of 100 percent, or an A.

In the Izzy-and-Frank scenario, Izzy had the following scores:

- Assignment one (project): 25/50 or 50 percent (F)

- Assignment two (midterm): 130/200 or 65 percent (D)

- Assignment three (paper): 25/50 or 50 percent (F)

- Assignment four (final exam): 130/200 or 65 percent (D)

- Assignment five (attendance and participation): 490/500 or 98 percent (A)

> *The mathematical method a teacher uses to determine a final grade is a mystery to many secondary students and their parents.*

- Izzy's total: 800/1,000 or 80 percent (B)

Frank earned the following:

- Assignment one (project): 50/50 or 100 percent (A)

- Assignment two (midterm): 160/200 or 80 percent (B)

- Assignment three (paper): 50/50 or 100 percent (A)

- Assignment four (final exam): 160/200 or 80 percent (B)

- Assignment five (attendance and participation): 370/500 or 68 percent (C)

- Frank's total: 790/1,000 or 79 percent (C)

I think it is easy to see why Frank is upset. He has an A average on his project and paper and a B average on his tests, whereas Izzy has an F average on her project and paper and a D average on her tests. Izzy's attendance and participation were very good. Frank was sick often and is shy, so he didn't say much during class discussions. Frank believes it was not his fault that he was sick. And although he knew the point distribution from the syllabus, he just didn't believe that saying a few things in class would matter all that much.

Frank's mom and dad aren't happy either. "How on earth can a student get A's on both assignments and B's on both tests and get a C for a final grade?" Frank's dad complains.

The answer is quite simple: Frank did not focus on the category that mattered most in terms of his final grade. Attendance and participation were worth 500 points, half the total points possible. Frank learned the hard way that often, a higher grade has nothing at all to do with knowledge, effort, or skill but rather understanding the simple mechanics of the grading system.

The Weighted Grade System

Weighted grading is the second most popular grading system among teachers. It works like this: The teacher assigns more final value to some assignments than to others. So 100 points on a test may not have the same value as 100 points on homework.

Here's an example to illustrate weighted grading. Mr. Weighty has set up his computer grading system to do the following calculations:

- 50 percent of the final grade will be derived from points earned on tests.

- 20 percent of the final grade will come from points earned via homework.

- 10 percent of the final grade will come from points earn on quizzes.

- 10 percent of the final grade will come from points earned through the final exam.

- 10 percent of the final grade will come from participation.

Let's say you've earned the following points:

- Tests: You receive 300 of 500 points, or 60 percent of the possible points. Sixty percent (0.6) multiplied by a weight of 50 percent (0.5) equals 30 percent (0.3).

- Homework: You receive 1,000 of 1,000 points, or 100 percent of the possible points. One hundred percent (1.0) multiplied by a weight of 20 percent (0.2) equals 20 percent (0.2).

- Quizzes: You receive 400 of 500 points, or 80 percent of the possible points. Eighty percent (0.8) multiplied by a weight of 10 percent (0.1) equals 8 percent (0.08).

- Final exam: You receive 120 of 200 points, or 60 percent of the possible points. Sixty percent (0.6) multiplied by a weight of 10 percent (0.1) equals 6 percent (0.06).

- Participation: You receive 90 of 100 points, or 90 percent of the possible points. Ninety percent (0.9) multiplied by a weight of 10 percent (0.1) equals 9 percent (0.09).

- Total: When you add up the parts of your grade (0.3 + 0.2 + 0.08 + 0.06 + 0.09), you get 0.73 or 73 percent. Your grade is a C.

Teacher Quirks

A teacher's quirks can play a role in grading, too. This may not be fair, but it does happen—so it helps to be aware of any quirks your teachers may sport. Consider the following example from my own experience.

I was in my senior year of college. I wanted to graduate early, but I needed a few more credits to make the final tally and get my degree. I wanted these credits to come from the history department, since that was my major, but I did not have the time or energy for tons of work or writing.

I started asking around: "Which professor whose class you've taken gives the least amount of work?" One student gave me an interesting answer: "You want Dr. Bigfoot—not because he gives the least amount of work, but because he has this weird quirk that few have discovered. If you know this quirk, you will get an A. But this information is going to cost you." I think this student was just being dramatic, but I took his point: the information was valuable and should be kept secret, because if it got out, the advantage would disappear.

What was the big secret in this case? And why was this professor known by the name Bigfoot? Well, Dr. Bigfoot had written a book on Bigfoot. His colleagues and students would constantly joke about this with puns, limericks, and innuendos. Some of the jokes were quite funny, but he hated them all. However, if you spoke to him with a sincere interest in his research on Bigfoot, when it came time to grade your work, he seemed to remember you in a more positive light. Your chances of getting an A were almost 100 percent.

ACTION PLAN

Use your teachers' grading systems and quirks to your advantage:

1. Create a simple spreadsheet or graphic organizer listing the names of your assignments, the points possible for each, and the points you receive. Keep running totals so that you know exactly where you stand and what a future assignment could do to your grade.

2. If a teacher uses a weighted grade system, be aware of the categories that carry the greatest weight. Prioritize your assignments by weight.

3. Avoid getting zeros on any assignments.

4. Know each of your teacher's quirks when it comes to grading. Successful people are observant. Academic failure is often due to a lack of awareness of the nuances found in teacher grading systems.

5. Think about these questions and discuss them with your classmates:

    • Do the final grades for Frank and Izzy seem fair to you? Why?

    • What could Frank have done to avoid getting a C?

    • What lessons can you derive from this scenario?

CHAPTER 20

Grade Destroyer Number Two: Lack of Class Participation

I've written this chapter, like the preceding one, to address students directly. You can use the information in this chapter as notes for a lecture. Or you could simply have your students read the chapter, then follow up the reading with a class discussion.

What Is Participation?

Many students are reluctant, for various reasons, to engage in class discussions. Are you one of them? If so, in terms of getting higher grades, it does not matter *why* you have not raised your hand and asked a question or made a comment. The fact is that you haven't participated, and your grade suffers because of it.

Participation begins with showing up, of course. You can't participate if you aren't there. It also means raising your hand, asking questions, and making comments. But it includes more, too. A participation grade also involves body language, attitude, tone of voice, and likability. It does not necessarily involve knowledge of the subject matter, a sharp and witty mind, or the ability to articulate knock-your-socks-off questions. (Although those contributions certainly don't hurt.) Rather, participation requires an awareness of when and how to act interested in what your teacher is saying. When you act interested, you validate your teacher's expertise and passion.

Acting interested and getting involved means being willing to learn with a pleasant attitude that is not phony. (Don't overdo it; remember, your teachers and fellow students are quite experienced in spotting fakery.) For example, I will never forget my college professor Dr. Bigfoot.

(See Chapter 19 for more on this interesting fellow.) Dr. Bigfoot was the history professor everyone wanted, because he was easy to read. He actually believed in Bigfoot. And he appreciated students who supported him instead of making fun of him. So during the several classes that I signed up to take with him over four years, I believed in Bigfoot, too. I figured out when to nod my head in agreement and when to look subtly disappointed at the doubters.

How to Participate

Is it too much to think that you can master the skill of acting interested without phoniness? Of course not—you already know how to play your family like a fiddle, right? It is time to direct that skill toward your school success.

In order to develop this skill, you need to study your teachers. It is worth the effort. It is neither time-consuming nor hard to do. Studying your teachers' quirks can help you achieve higher grades—both by boosting your participation score and by helping you gain more knowledge in the process. And of course, this approach is more interesting than just zoning out every day during class.

> A participation grade also involves body language, attitude, tone of voice, and likability. It does not necessarily involve knowledge of the subject matter, a sharp and witty mind, or the ability to articulate knock-your-socks-off questions.

Observe your teachers with the goal of understanding them. What are they passionate about? What types of student responses make them smile (or try not to smile)? When and why do they get irritated? When is the best time to approach them? Can they handle being challenged, or do they always have to be right? Do they laugh or do they get angry when something unexpected happens? Do they notice good behavior? Are they quick to judge?

Dedicate an area in your general notebook to your teacher studies. Title this section with something like "Personality Observations." In this part of your notebook, make one small section for each of your teachers. Once your notebook is organized this way, jot down your observations about what gets positive and negative reactions from your teachers.

For example, you might note: "Ms. Morningstar—wait till she's had coffee before asking questions." Or: "Mr. Halitosis is a close talker and can never give a simple, one-word answer. Note to self: don't give him a sour look, and be prepared to look interested for about five minutes." Or: "Mrs. Straycat believes she can save all the wayward children. Note to self: tell her how much she has changed your life." Lastly: "Mr. Cadetcore categorizes his students as slackers, workers, and space cadets. Note to self: sit next to the workers, turn in your work promptly, and look alert by having good body language."

> Studying your teachers' quirks can help you achieve higher grades—both by boosting your participation score and by helping you gain more knowledge in the process. And of course, this approach is more interesting than just zoning out every day during class.

Once you understand your teachers' personalities, it's easier to be a likable student. But why is it important to be likable? You may have heard that teachers don't have favorites. That is complete bunk. Teachers are human, and humans have favorites. Of course, teachers will say that this never affects their grading, but sometimes it does. That's because grading is a subjective judgment—an opinion that teachers offer based on some calculations that they control. All the categories that contribute to a final grade have some element of subjectivity. That means you need to make a good impression with your teacher in order to maximize your scores and get the best possible grade.

If you are not a teacher's favorite student, there's no need to change your personality. (That's not really possible anyway, nor is it a good idea.) But you *can* observe how to act prudently around that teacher. Just exercise self-control and humility. Refrain from singing your own praises, and avoid giving the impression that you feel that you are God's gift to teachers. This is great practice for life in the real world.

ACTION PLAN

Get the most out of your class participation grade with the following tips:

1. Greet your teachers when you see them each day. Do so naturally, not like you're sucking up.

2. Observe and record your teachers' reactions to topics and people. Avoid what brings on negative reactions in favor of what generates positive reactions.

3. Ask questions and make appropriate comments during lectures. Do this no matter how shy you feel. Reward yourself each time you speak up, if necessary, to keep doing it regularly.

4. Avoid arrogance. Participate in a way that shows your interest, not in a way that highlights your huge ego and your vast knowledge.

5. Don't talk so much that you get a reputation as being Phony Phil, Browniepoint Betsy, or Pick-Me Pat.

6. Use alert body language. Pay attention. Face the teacher, not another student. Look interested in the discussion of the dangling participle even if you would rather take that dangling thing and hang yourself with it.

7. At the end of group work, help put the room back in order. This small effort can build a lot of goodwill with teachers.

8. Think about these questions and discuss them with your classmates:

   • Do you agree with the definition of participation in this chapter? If so, why? If not, why?

   • What do you think of the idea of dedicating part of your notebook to teacher observations?

   • What do you do to get participation points? How successful are you? Explain.

   • Do teachers really have favorites? How can this fact work to your advantage?

   • What lessons can you take away from this chapter?

CHAPTER 21

Grade Destroyer Number Three: Study What?

This chapter, like the preceding two, is written to address students directly. You can use the following information as notes for a lecture. Or you could simply have your students read the chapter, then follow up the reading with a class discussion.

Destination: Test

If I had a dollar for every time a student claimed to have studied for a test but complained that it did not help at all, I would have retired in 1990. I've found that most students simply want the time they spend studying to translate into higher grades. But this often does not happen—at least not at first. Why? There could be several reasons, but here's an important one: studying needs the right *destination* in order to be productive.

Study is most productive when its *destination* is the assessment—when you are studying in order to do well on the test. This means your success depends largely on knowing exactly what is likely to be on the actual test. Many teachers directly or indirectly try to hide this fact—as well as what material the test will cover. Whether this hiding is ethical is another question entirely. But it is common. Let me reassure you that it is ethical for you as a student to try to anticipate test types, materials, and questions so that you can study effectively. Of course, this is true only if you're not looking at the test itself. Doing that is cheating, plain and simple.

How can a student find out what is on a test in an ethical way when the teacher intentionally or unintentionally obscures this information? First, it helps to know that a test may come from one of three possible sources:

1. The teacher creates the test using nothing but the teacher's own notes and knowledge.

2. The teacher creates the test using the Internet or questions provided by the textbook publishers.

3. Combo platter: The teacher uses both methods.

Ask the Teacher

The easiest way to determine the teacher's test-making method is to ask the teacher. For example, you might say, "Do you make your tests yourself, or do you use the textbook publishers and the Internet to come up with those good questions?" With any luck, you'll get a straight answer. Press your teacher if you get an answer that's too general or too vague—but not to the point of irritation, of course.

Teacher-Created Test Questions

Your teacher might reply, "Well, Johnny B. Inquisitive, I make up questions myself based on what I cover in class." Bingo! Now you know where to find the test material.

Listen in class like your life depends on it. Notice when this teacher starts harping on a particular subject or says, "Okay, now this is interesting," or, "No one seems to remember this." Maybe your teacher lingers on a point or changes tone or smiles while talking about a topic. That means this topic will probably be on the test. If you are paying attention, then you'll see the signs telling you what's important. Make a special mark in your notes when you see these signs. In other words, don't be lazy; write down what the teacher says *and* does.

> You don't need to know exactly what is on a test word for word. You must, however, figure out what types of details or concepts the teacher will hold you accountable for.

After you receive the first test back from this teacher, examine the types of questions it contains. Why? Because by doing so, you can gain insight on this teacher's testing style. A particular teacher's tests will often follow the same pattern. For example, a teacher may like vocabulary. A teacher may focus on practical uses for the information or may fixate on cause and effect. Look for the patterns by comparing tests as they are returned to you over the course of a semester. If possible, talk to previous students. They may have some insight on this teacher's testing quirks.

Ready-Made Test Questions

Many teachers use ready-made test questions, especially for multiple-choice tests, by cutting and pasting them from a publisher's test bank CD or from a website. If you know that is how the teacher makes the test, then you can preview the source. It is good practice to try some of these questions.

There is probably nothing more frustrating than to study and study and still do poorly on the test. If this happens, your failure is more of an indication that you studied the wrong information than that you don't or can't understand the material.

Some sources on the Web have released standardized test questions for state tests such as California's CST (California Standards Test) and CAHSEE (California High School Exit Examination), as well as for national tests (ACT, SAT, AP). Simply type into your favorite search engine something like "U.S. history released questions," and you'll find these questions easily. These released questions are supposedly field-tested, validity-tested, norm-tested, animal-tested, childproofed, low-fat, and organic.

The publishers of your textbook very likely have one or more websites—for students and/or for teachers—where you can find topics for study if your teacher creates tests from publisher-provided material. On these websites, you will probably be able to see some samples of the actual questions that your teacher uses. Believe or it not, textbook publishers often use the same or similar questions on the student section of their website as they do on the teacher section. What is more: it is easy to get on the teacher section and get access to all the teacher resources. Publishers don't ask for any teacher credentials; often they simply require you to create a name and a password.

Examine the First Test

If the teacher refuses to tell you how the test is made, don't panic. You can figure it out. When you receive your first test back, examine the format and ask yourself:

1. Do these questions have anything to do with the reading?

2. Do these questions have anything to do with the lectures?

3. Do these questions have anything to do with the work this teacher has given?

4. Do these questions have anything to do with vocabulary?

The answers to these four questions will tell you what to study. Here's how:

1. If the answer to question one is yes, read and read and read some more. Pay attention to how the teacher creates questions from the reading. Are the questions about concepts or details? What kind of concepts? What kind of details?

2. If the answer to question two is yes, listen closely in class and keep good notes. Study how the teacher creates questions from the lectures. What clues does the teacher give during lectures that what's being said could be a test question? Does the teacher laugh? Hesitate? What does the teacher's body language say? Mark your observations in your notes. When you get the test back, look at your notes and try to see a pattern linking your teacher's lectures and tests.

3. If the answer to question three is yes, keep all your work for the class so that you can review it. And you'd better not be copying that work, because your chance of remembering copied work will be low.

4. If the answer to question four is yes, study the vocabulary from the book and the assigned work.

You don't need to know exactly what is on a test word for word. You must, however, figure out what types of details or concepts the teacher will hold you accountable for. The clues are there, even if the teacher won't tell you directly. Imagine that you are a detective hired to discover this person's methods, and you will get paid a million dollars for figuring them out. Do you think you could do it? Of course you could—especially for such a big reward! And this reward isn't actually far from reality. Over time, good grades could save you and make you a lot of money. Think about why I say that. Scholarships and financial aid are not generally given to C students. Employers are not looking for average performers. If you do well with grades, you are telling the world, "I am smart enough to understand the game of life and hardworking enough to win at it. Therefore, I will be successful in college or in this job."

> Study is most productive when its **destination** is the assessment—when you are studying in order to do well on the test. This means your success depends largely on knowing exactly what is likely to be on the actual test.

There is probably nothing more frustrating than to study and study and still do poorly on the test. If this happens, your failure is more of an indication that you studied the wrong information than that you don't or can't understand the material. Figure out what the right information is. Use all the resources available to you as you investigate your teacher's test-making methods. Talk to other teachers and students for clues if necessary. Do whatever it takes (within the bounds of decency, of course), and don't give up until you crack the case.

ACTION PLAN

1. If your goal is higher grades, direct your study toward the test. Find out as much about the test format and topics as you can.

2. If the test is teacher-created, take detailed notes and study them. When the test is returned, notice what types of information become test questions.

3. If the test questions come from the textbook publishers, preview the test online if possible. Remember, even if it is not the exact same test that your teacher uses, it will probably be similar—and therefore full of helpful clues for you.

4. If your teacher won't tell you how he or she creates tests, figure it out for yourself by examining the first test when you receive it back.

5. Use flash cards to review the topics that most likely will be on the test. Focus on information you have difficulty remembering.

6. Think about these questions and discuss them with your classmates:

   • Do you agree with this chapter's description of what studying really is? Why or why not?

   • What do you think of the idea of investigating how your teacher creates tests? Is this a good idea? Why or why not?

   • Why do some students study for days and still do poorly on tests?

   • Do you agree with the following advice? "Learn what is on the test and then study accordingly."

   • What lessons can you take away from this chapter?

CHAPTER 22

Grade Destroyer Number Four: The X Factor

This chapter, like the three before it, is written to address students directly. You can use the following information as notes for a lecture. Or you could simply have your students read the chapter, then follow up the reading with a class discussion.

What Is the X Factor?

The X factor is extra-credit work—or, more accurately, *not doing* extra-credit work when it's offered. Most teachers offer extra credit. Perhaps it is a good idea. Perhaps it is not. Nevertheless, it is an opportunity that most students do not utilize fully. In fact, many do not use it at all. Rabbi and writer Max Forman observed that "education seems to be in America the only commodity of which the consumer tries to get as little as he can from his money." I think Forman was right. It seems to me that many students will do only what their teachers absolutely require of them.

Students often see extra credit in the wrong light—as work that should be done only if they need to make up for a past mistake. On the contrary: if higher grades are your goal, then extra credit is work that you should always do.

You probably know a few students with incredible GPAs. Do you ever wonder, "How did they do it?" The answer is likely quite simple: they did all or most of the extra credit offered. On the flip side, you probably also know plenty of bright, well-spoken, and engaging students with average or below-average GPAs. Why don't they have higher grades? Again, the answer is likely quite simple: they did not take advantage of the extra-credit opportunities their teachers presented.

The Power of Extra Credit

Don't believe me? Take a look at the power of extra credit in terms of its mathematical impact on a grade.

Scenario One

Student A achieves 790 of 1,000 possible points this semester. That's 79 percent, or a grade of C. He decides to do a ten-point, one-hour extra-credit assignment. He earns all ten points and raises his total to 800 of 1,000. That's 80 percent, or a grade of B. He is able to do this because with extra credit, only the number of points earned (the first number in a student's score) changes. Because extra credit is not required work, the number of points possible (the second number in a student's score) doesn't change. With required assignments, both numbers change.

Why am I telling you this story? Here is why: a small amount of extra credit can make a big difference in your final grade. In the case above, Student A's extra-credit work raised his overall score one percentage point, which turned his grade from a C into a B. If that extra-credit assignment had been a required assignment, Student A would have ended up with 800 of 1,010 possible points, or 79.2 percent—still a C.

See the difference extra credit can make? Extra credit is the fastest way to bring up your grade. Even if you do terrible work on an extra-credit assignment, whatever points you earn can only help you, not hurt you.

Scenario Two

Student B has 900 of 1,000 possible points going into the final exam, which is worth another 100 points. Here's the problem: she struggles with multiple-choice tests, and the final will be a multiple-choice test. She always studies the wrong things and always blows the exam. Now she has a decision to make.

- Plan A: She could study for the test the same way she always does.

- Plan B: She could complete a report worth 50 extra-credit points, using the same amount of time as Plan A would take.

What would you do? Let's play both plans out based on the most likely result:

- Plan A: The student studies for the final exam in the only way she knows how and scores the same way she usually does. She earns 60 of 100 possible points. So her final grade is 960 of 1,100 possible points, or 87.3 percent (B).

- Plan B: The student does the extra credit and does not study at all for the test. She earns all 50 extra-credit points and scores 50 of 100 possible points on the test. Her final score is 1,000 of 1,100 possible points. That's 90.9 percent, or a grade of A.

This is not the place to discuss the value of extra credit when it comes to learning or mastering content. Nor is this the place to discuss the validity of the teacher's grading system. This is the place to understand the math that is used to make your grade. And here's the bottom line: if a teacher offers extra credit, you should jump on it—no excuses.

Excuses, Excuses

Some students may hesitate to take on extra credit for any number of reasons. They feel they don't have the time for it. They're too busy. They can't do a good job on it. They do enough work already. Extra credit is just a bunch of extra work for little reward. Their grade is fine; extra credit is only to make up for missing or failed assignments. The list of misconceptions is a long one.

> *Extra credit is for everybody. There is no risk in doing extra-credit work. The results are secure; they can only help you.*

If you are thinking along those lines, please change your attitude. It is not in your best interest to ignore the positive impact extra credit can have on your final grade. In addition, doing extra work for a class sends a helpful message to your teacher. When you go beyond the minimum requirements, you are showing your teacher that you care about learning. You show that you are willing to do whatever it takes to be successful. Extra-credit work is time well spent. It buys you negotiation power for the future. It does so because successful negotiation is rooted in what you have done, not what you say you will do. When you complete extra credit, you are acting and not just talking. You now have a reputation to point to, and that makes people listen to you.

Extra credit is for everybody. There is no risk in doing extra-credit work. The results are secure; they can only help you. When you study for a test—even for days upon days—you can't be sure how you'll do. By contrast, when you turn in extra credit, your grade goes up. It's as simple as that.

Consider extra credit as an academic insurance policy you cannot afford to be without, because sometimes life happens. You never know when you might encounter an unexpected obstacle and need those spare points.

ACTION PLAN

1. Always embrace the opportunity to earn extra credit. Extra-credit work can only help—never hurt—your grade.

2. Ask your teacher for extra credit early in the semester. This shows your good attitude and boosts your score right off the bat.

3. Present your teacher with an extra-credit plan to research a topic that interests you and that the teacher feels is worthwhile. This way, your teacher will see that you are taking the initiative, and you will enjoy doing the work.

4. Think about the following questions and discuss them with your classmates:

   • Can you explain the impact extra credit has on your grade?

   • What parts of this chapter are confusing to you?

   • Do you personally always attempt extra credit? Why or why not?

   • Do you agree that if a teacher offers extra credit, you should jump on it?

   • What lessons can you take away from this chapter?

CHAPTER 23

Grade Destroyer Number Five: Zero Tolerance

This chapter, like the four before it, is written to address students directly. You can use the following information as notes for a lecture. Or you could simply have your students read the chapter, then follow up the reading with a class discussion.

A Tolerance for Zeros

Known as the Black Death, the bubonic plague of the 14th century reportedly decimated one-third of the population of Europe. Did you know there is a highly contagious Academic Black Plague of the 21st century? What is that plague? Well, getting just one zero on an assignment will infect a student's GPA to potential death. This may seem unbelievable, but it's true.

I've had plenty of students contract this plague. In fact, about one-third of the students in any given class might already be infected. Some are unaware of how easy it is to catch. They don't see the devastation a zero on an assignment will do to their final grade. They have zero tolerance—a tolerance for zeros.

Frannie Forgetful can help us illustrate this problem. She is quite bright, but sometimes she forgets to turn in an assignment. (This is not unusual. Almost every student fails to turn in one or two assignments over the course of a semester. The reasons are many and varied.) Frannie's forgetfulness destroys her final grade for the class. When Frannie finally realizes what has happened, she is shocked. She feels as though a virus has attacked her hard drive and ruined everything she worked on all semester.

Understanding the Math

Frannie needs to pay attention to the math involved in calculating her final grade. To understand this math, let's look at some common student scenarios. Frannie is a good example of the uninformed student in scenario one.

Scenario One: The Bright but Uninformed Student

The uniformed student does not comprehend the devastation of a zero. Here are her scores:

Assignment	Points	Percentage	Grade
1	90/100	90%	A
2	90/100	90%	A
3	90/100	90%	A
4	80/100	80%	B
5	90/100	90%	A
6	0/100	0%	F
7	90/100	90%	A
8	80/100	80%	B
9	0/100	0%	F
10	90/100	90%	A
11	80/100	80%	B
12	0/100	0%	F
13	90/100	90%	A
14	80/100	80%	B
15	90/100	90%	A
Final grade	1,040/1,500	69.3%	D

Did you notice that this student got just three zeros out of fifteen assignments? At first glance, this student looks like an A or B student. She did high-quality work for most of her assignments; she earned eight A's, four B's, and three F's. But her zeros dragged her grade all the way down to a D.

Scenario Two: The Very Lazy but Informed Student

Now let's replace those zeros with some really poor-quality, half-baked, last-minute work and see what happens:

Assignment	Points	Percentage	Grade
1	90/100	90%	A
2	90/100	90%	A
3	90/100	90%	A
4	80/100	80%	B
5	90/100	90%	A
6	25/100	25%	F
7	90/100	90%	A
8	80/100	80%	B
9	25/100	25%	F
10	90/100	90%	A
11	80/100	80%	A
12	25/100	25%	F
13	90/100	90%	A
14	80/100	80%	B
15	90/100	90%	A
Final grade	1,115/1,500	74.3%	C

This student got Fs on three assignments, but the Fs weren't zeros. He earned a few points for his work, even though it was of very low quality. Those points made a final grade of C possible.

Scenario Three: The Somewhat Lazy but Informed Student

Now let's try the same math with some D-quality work. Most students can get a D without much effort:

Assignment	Points	Percentage	Grade
1	90/100	90%	A
2	90/100	90%	A
3	90/100	90%	A
4	80/100	80%	B
5	90/100	90%	A

6	65/100	65%	D
7	90/100	90%	A
8	80/100	80%	B
9	65/100	65%	D
10	90/100	90%	A
11	80/100	80%	B
12	65/100	65%	D
13	90/100	90%	A
14	80/100	80%	B
15	90/100	90%	A
Final grade	1,235/1,500	82.3%	B

Once again, a little effort made a big difference in the student's final grade.

Scenario Four: The Not-So-Lazy and Informed Student

Now finally, let's try the math with some C work and one extra-credit assignment worth 100 points:

Assignment	Points	Percentage	Grade
1	90/100	90%	A
2	90/100	90%	A
3	90/100	90%	A
4	80/100	80%	B
5	90/100	90%	A
6	70/100	70%	C
7	90/100	90%	A
8	80/100	80%	B
9	70/100	70%	C
10	90/100	90%	A
11	80/100	80%	B
12	70/100	70%	C
13	90/100	90%	A

14	80/100	80%	B
15	90/100	90%	A
Extra credit	100/100	100%	A
Final grade	1,350/1,500	90%	A

This is quite a difference! After showing this math to many students, I have asked them, "What do you think?" I often get the following responses:

- "I did not turn in the assignment because I thought an F was an F."

- "I did not have time to do the assignment correctly so I decided not to do it at all."

- "How could not turning in a few assignments do that? That's crazy!"

- "I had no idea that a zero could change my grade so much."

Well, now you know. Use this knowledge to develop zero tolerance for getting zeros.

ACTION PLAN

1. Keep a running tally of your assignments. Do everything you can to avoid zeros. Remember, not all Fs are created equal.

2. If you've already got a zero, fix it by doing some extra credit. Ask for extra credit if necessary.

3. Think about the following questions and discuss them with your classmates:

   - Can you explain the impact getting a zero has on your grade?

   - What parts of this chapter are confusing to you?

   - Do you get zeros on assignments? Why?

   - What lessons can you take away from this chapter?

CHAPTER 24

Grade Destroyer Number Six: Late Work

I've written this chapter, like the five before it, to address students directly. You can use the following information as notes for a lecture. Or you could simply have your students read the chapter, then follow up the reading with a class discussion.

Teacher Attitudes Toward Late Work

Teachers have widely varying attitudes toward late work. Some educators think that late work should never be allowed. Some accept late work only in rare situations, such as a death in the family. On the other end of the spectrum are educators who levy virtually no penalty at all for late work. They feel that if the work was worth assigning in the first place, then it is worth doing. They think that it is better to have done the work and to have learned something than to skip it and miss the opportunity to learn.

Most instructors lie somewhere between these extremes. In my own circles, it seems that more and more teachers are leaning toward not accepting late work. If they allow work to be turned in late, they do so only by district mandate. In other words, many teachers accept only an excused absence as an acceptable reason for turning in an assignment late. That usually means a student has twenty-four to forty-eight hours after the absence to turn in the work—no ifs, ands, or buts.

Getting Credit for Late Work

How can you persuade a teacher to accept your late work? Try one of the following approaches.

The Flat-Out-Honest Approach

If you have a legitimate reason for turning in your work after the deadline, then explain that reason to your teacher as humbly and honestly as you can. Honesty combined with humility make a powerful recipe for persuading a teacher to bend the rules. Make your teacher believe you—after all, you are telling the truth. Appeal to your teacher's sense of compassion. You might couple your approach with an apologetic and sad demeanor, if you think this will work with your teacher's personality. But avoid acting phony at all costs. Avoid acting entitled, too. If you act as if your teacher owes you this consideration, then your chances of success will be severely diminished.

The I-Had-to-Deal-with-Things-out-of-My-Control Approach

Over the years, I've come to realize that many students deal with unbelievably difficult circumstances at home. But quite frankly, not all teachers are aware of this. For instance, some of your teachers may have no idea that you are playing the role of mother, father, babysitter, counselor, and caregiver to your siblings or other family members. Tell your teacher what's going on at home. Your teacher knows that life happens—to all of us. And sometimes things happen that are out of your control.

> *If you can remind your teachers of your common humanity in a polite, respectful way, you may move them. Sincerity, honesty, and humility are powerful, no matter how often they are used. These traits never get old, and they are never inappropriate.*

The Written-Apology-with-Completed-Assignment Approach

If you've finished the work but it's already late, you're better off trying to turn it in than not trying at all. To increase your chances of success, write one of the following notes to your teacher (in your own words, of course).

▶ Dear Mr. Moreno,

I am very sorry that I failed to turn in your last assignment. There was incredible drama in my house last week. (Describe it here, but don't go on about it too long; your teacher is busy.) I know that you do not have to give me any points at all for this assignment based on your syllabus and clear instructions, but I am turning this in so that you can see that I really did the work. I just did not want you to think that I am a slacker all the time.

Thanks,

Jasper

Dear Ms. Smith,

I am very sorry that I failed to complete your assignment on time. I sometimes let things distract me. There is no excuse for that, I know, but I am not giving up, and I made myself do your work to teach myself a lesson. I know that I am not getting points for it, but I wanted you to see that I am trying to be a serious student and person.

Sincerely,

Sarah

Why bother with this approach if you are going to get no points at all? Well, of course, the hope is that your teacher will buy what you are selling, and you *will* get points. We live in a world full of rude and lazy people, so any effort at being polite and hardworking is often rewarded—despite the letter of the law.

Even if you do not get any points, your effort will still pay off in the future. It is in no way a waste of your time. Remember the importance of likability. A polite, humble, and honest conversation with your teacher increases your likability. In addition, by doing the assignment you are probably learning something that will be on the test later. And it is never too late to build good habits. Completing your work is a great habit to cultivate.

Never fail to do late work just because there is a point deduction for lateness. Do not say to yourself, "Well, if I turn it in now, I will only get 50 percent of the points—so forget it. I am not doing it for half credit." If that's your attitude, change it now. Points are points, and all points are worthwhile. For a refresher course on this topic, review Chapter 23. It shows the absolute devastation a zero has on your grade. You can never afford a zero.

The I-Didn't-Know-What-to-Do Approach

I can't tell you how many students I've witnessed fail to do their work because they simply did not understand what the heck they were supposed to do. This is especially common in math. Ignorance is no excuse for failing to obey the law—and it's no excuse for failing to do your work either. If you honestly did not understand what to do, you may buy some time if you say or write the following (in your own words):

Dear Mr. Patel,

I stayed up until four a.m. trying to figure out your homework. If you doubt me, please email my mother, and she can verify that I'm telling the truth. I also called both Kelly Q. and Kim C. for help, and they can also testify that I tried. Today in advisory someone finally explained the work to me in a way that I get. I am willing to do double the work if you would accept it. Perhaps you can take some points off if you like, but here is the work to show you that I am trying.

Sincerely,

Will

Humanity, Honesty, and Humility

Do you see a common thread in all four of these approaches? They are all appeals to your teacher's humanity. Hopefully, your teacher is not hardened by continuous excuses and does not automatically tune you out. Life happens to everyone, so we can assume that your teacher has been in your position and will treat you as she or he would like to be treated.

If you can remind your teachers of your common humanity in a polite, respectful way, you may move them. Sincerity, honesty, and humility are powerful, no matter how often they are used. These traits never get old, and they are never inappropriate.

A word of caution: Do not wait too long to offer up late work. In other words, don't wait until the last week of the semester to make your move, because at that point you will have lost all credibility. Your teacher may think that if it really mattered to you, and you really had a legitimate excuse, you would have addressed the problem much sooner. Deal with late work as soon as possible.

ACTION PLAN

1. If your work is late through no fault of your own, then explain your situation to your teacher in the humblest way possible. If your teacher is unmoved, then enlist help from the office or your parents. If you can get an officially excused absence, then you can remind your teacher of school policy regarding excused absences and late work. If the office is of no help, your parents could step in. Teachers like to avoid negative discussions with parents.

2. Try writing your teacher a short note to win time or favor. A note serves as a tangible reminder to address your problem, and it prevents the possibility that you may attempt a face-to-face discussion at the wrong time.

3. Always do late work, even if you will get only partial credit for it. Some points are better than no points.

4. Think about the following questions and discuss them with your classmates:

   • Can you explain the impact late work has on your grade?

   • What parts of this chapter are confusing to you?

   • Do you turn in late work? Why or why not?

   • Do you think that the letters in this chapter would work on your teachers? Explain.

   • What lessons can you take away from this chapter?

CHAPTER 25

Grade Destroyer Number Seven: Unlikability

This chapter, like the six before it, is written to address students directly. You can use the text that follows as your notes for a lecture. Or you could simply have your students read this chapter, then follow up the reading with a class discussion.

Unlikable vs. Likable Behavior

Which of the following four approaches often experienced by teachers do you think will have the best chance of getting a positive response?

The You-Owe-Me Approach

"Hey, Mr. Chen. I noticed that I am at 89.9 percent. You are going to raise that for me, aren't you? I mean, it is me we are talking about, right? You know that I am your favorite, right? Remember that test? You owe me two points. Just give it to me now, and I'll forgive you. I know you'll do the right thing. You know I deserve it."

What is Mr. Chen thinking right now? Something along these lines: "_____." (This text has been edited for inappropriate language.) The you–owe–me approach rarely works. In fact, it usually just ticks off teachers. Avoid it in all its forms.

The Forgetful-Teacher Approach

"Hi, Ms. Sidibe. I noticed that I am at 89.9 percent. I was just wondering if you counted all that extra credit I did? Actually, did you remember to give me those points for Jeopardy? How come Kaya got twelve points and I only got eleven on the last project? Did you remember . . . what about . . . how about . . . ?"

What is Ms. Sidibe thinking right now? Something like: "_____." (This text has also been edited for inappropriate language.) This approach assumes that the problem is with how the teacher does things. An injustice has been perpetrated on the poor student. The teacher forgot to give all the points. This teacher-blaming approach, like the you-owe-me approach, rarely works. Don't try it, because you'll probably just make your situation worse.

The Ego-Inflating Approach

"Hi, Mr. Sells. I noticed that I am at 89.9 percent. I am a little disappointed at getting 89.9 percent, because I really do love your class and have learned so much. You are the best teacher that I have ever had. My parents are going to kill me if I don't get an A, because they think that you are the best, too. You are the greatest . . . you are so . . . you are the . . . !"

What is Mr. Sells thinking right now? Probably: "_____." (More inappropriate language.) Although the ego-inflating approach is better than the previous two approaches, it still does not usually work. Most teachers have heard this kind of flattery so often that they know it is insincere.

The Grateful-Student Approach

"Hi, Ms. Grady. I noticed that I am at 89.9 percent. I had an A before, but that last test really killed me. I should have studied longer on the American Revolution. I was overconfident or something. I am bringing this up because I feel that I do understand what you were teaching. I would be willing to do anything to demonstrate that I have mastered the objectives for this course at a high level. I know that grades should reflect what students have learned and the work they have done. I was thinking that I could do some sort of project on the American Revolution to bring up my skills in that area to the level required for an A."

> *This approach puts no blame or pressure on the teacher. It shows an awareness of the specific problem, the ability to think critically, a concern about the class objectives, and a willingness to work hard.*

What is Ms. Grady thinking right now? It's a safe bet that she's not swearing under her breath. The student clearly understands that a grade is not a gift and wants to earn it. The student believes that a higher grade will be an honest and ethical reflection of ability and effort. The student knows that he or she alone is responsible for a lower-than-expected grade and is grateful for the opportunity to fix it. This is a better approach than the

> *Likability can be cultivated. You may not be born gifted with charm, but you can still be likable. And you can always get better at it.*

other three because it puts no blame or pressure on the teacher. It shows an awareness of the specific problem, the ability to think critically, a concern about the class objectives, and a willingness to work hard. This is different from doing work as if it is a hoop-jumping contest for a grade. This type of attitude is rare in students; it is sure to get Ms. Grady's attention.

Angela's Story

I once had a student I'll call Angela who was constantly on my case to raise her current grade a point here or a point there. Did this endless prodding annoy me? Normally it would have, but Angela's approach was so likable that it didn't bother me at all. Every time she came to check on her grade, she was polite and humble and oh-so-grateful.

Angela wanted an A so badly that even the teacher next door could see her persistence. Because she asked about her grade so often, I would always tell her that her score was 89.9 percent—whether that was true or not. Eventually I told her that if she asked again, I would change her name to "89.9 Percent" and call her that in front of everyone for the rest of the year.

Angela barely made it one day before she asked about her grade again. I kept my word. Her new name did not offend or deter her. She just kept on doing her best, asking about her grade, and being a likable person. It was hard for me not to show that she was one of my favorite students that year.

I believe that when Angela's teachers saw her, none of them thought, "Here comes that pain in the butt again to ask about her grade." On the contrary, they probably smiled. Angela was difficult to dislike. Perhaps it was her sense of humor. Perhaps it was her determination in the face of great apathy among her peers. Perhaps it was her willingness to do whatever it might take to change her grade. Her intellectual abilities were average. But her likability was far above average. Students like Angela do more for improving the profession of teaching than 100 university courses could.

On the last day of school, she gave me a framed plaque that said:

> AN EXCELLENT TEACHER WHO HAS TAUGHT US
> WISDOM THROUGHOUT THE YEARS
>
> THANK YOU FOR YOUR DEDICATION
>
> 89.9 PERCENT

How does Angela's story end? She was accepted to several of America's elite universities. She earned a bachelor's degree and has an excellent job in Riverside, California.

Angela praised my teaching, but I have to say that she taught me far more than I ever taught her. Among other things, I think Angela shows that academic success involves more than just natural abilities. All of us have the power to choose our own academic destinies.

Cultivating Likability

Likability can be cultivated. You may not be born gifted with charm, but you can still be likable. And you can always get better at it. Remember that getting the highest grades possible depends to a large extent on your relationship with your teachers. Observe your teachers and try to understand them. Never play the phony. Be yourself, but think before you talk. Ask yourself, "If I were the teacher, how would I respond to what I am about to say or do?" Fast-forward your plan to the end to see if your approach is likely to produce the desired results.

You may be thinking, "Really, I am just not that likable a person. What am I supposed to do?" The action plan that follows describes several tools you can use to cultivate likability. Don't underestimate its power. It covers a multitude of mistakes. It will help your teacher, your friends, and your future boss or spouse be more patient with you. Likability will give you a critical boost to help you achieve your goals.

ACTION PLAN

1. Put the blame for a problem on yourself, even if you believe it is not your fault. If it is not your fault and you take responsibility anyway, the teacher will know it and will respect you.

2. If a problem is your fault, demonstrate an awareness of what you did wrong.

3. Offer a specific plan—one that is not a slacker hoop-jumping exercise—to get the points you need. Go way above what you think is fair in your offer. Show your willingness and commitment to work your butt off for your grade.

4. Show gratitude, humility, and good manners. Say, "Thank you." Say, "I appreciate it very much." Say, "I am sorry." Say, "I am willing."

5. Never demand an action.

6. Never threaten to go over your teacher's head. Even if you win that battle, you will lose the war of higher grades because your teacher will dislike you from then on.

7. Leave the entitled attitude at home.

8. When appropriate, remind your teacher of the intangibles that you add to the class, such as your group leadership, your participation, your interest level that sets a nice class tone, and your past diligence. But don't play your own fiddle too long; let others praise you more than you praise yourself.

9. Make sure that you speak to your teacher more often than just when you want something. Talk with your teacher all year long, so that when it comes time to discuss your grade, he or she does not get the impression that all you really care about is yourself.

CHAPTER 26

Grade Destroyer Number Eight: Procrastination

Just like the seven previous chapters, this one addresses students directly. Use the following information as notes for a lecture, or simply have your students read the chapter and then follow up the reading with a class discussion.

A Portrait of Procrastination

I think procrastination is one of the biggest stumbling blocks that trip up students on the road to academic success and higher grades. The temptation to procrastinate is part of human nature, and procrastination is especially tempting when the task at hand is unpleasant. People think, "Ugh, I can't stand the thought of doing this. If I wait long enough, maybe this awful job will disappear." But of course, it never disappears. It just gets more and more awful.

Case Study

On Monday I post on the homework board, word for word, the history essay prompt that I will use for Friday's in-class essay. I tell my students that preparing for this essay is their entire homework assignment for the week.

On Thursday I poll the class of forty students to see how many of them have done anything with this assignment. Only five have even thought about it seriously. Now the whining, begging, and deal-making begins. Thirty-five sad faces plead for a delay until Monday. Why? They waited until the last minute to prepare for the essay, and now they feel overwhelmed.

I say, "No, the essay will be on Friday. Poor planning on your part does not constitute an emergency on my part." They hate me. So be it; I have done my job. I will not reinforce poor work habits. The next day, several students tell me that they stayed up past midnight. They seem to think I will be impressed. But poor planning and procrastination is not impressive to me.

> *The chain of events that procrastination triggers never ends well. Procrastination almost always creates more work for you in the long run.*

Let's pretend that you are one of the procrastinators in my class. I can think of at least five possible reasons why your procrastination was a terrible idea:

1. The assignment required two to three hours of reading and preparation with a clear mind. You gave it one hour, from midnight to one o'clock in the morning. You probably will not pass this essay, because you are not a naturally gifted writer, and your only hope was to prepare for it thoroughly.

2. You are now so tired that you are about as alert as a sloth. Consequently, the test you have in your science class today will also suffer.

3. You decided to prioritize, and that meant you did no math homework last night. Your math grade now suffers, and you are lost in math class for the rest of the year. (This actually happened to me in ninth grade.)

4. You overslept and missed your first period, English class, and didn't turn in your homework. Your English grade is now shot, because that teacher does not accept late work under any circumstances. The extra-sad thing is: you did the work.

5. You fail the history essay as expected. You get a poor work notice in the mail for history, English, math, and science. Your dad takes your cell phone. You are so mad and bored and humiliated that you feel like dropping out of school here and now.

Okay, maybe I'm exaggerating just a *little*. But hopefully my hyperbole sends you a strong message: don't procrastinate! The chain of events that procrastination triggers never ends well. Procrastination almost always creates more work for you in the long run. Meditate on that. Do you really want to be in the habit of working harder than you need to all the time?

Kicking the Procrastination Habit

Procrastination breeds more procrastination. So what can you do to kick the habit?

Students often attempt to complete the homework that is least dreadful first, and then they move on to the most painful work last. This is a form of procrastination, and it is a huge mistake academically. If you want higher grades, then you must concentrate your efforts on the work that affects your grade the most. For example, if your dreadful pain-in-the-butt algebra homework will help you pass the test tomorrow, then do that work first, when your mind is at its sharpest. It does not matter that you hate algebra. Logic dictates that you will get more bang for your buck by giving this particular assignment top priority.

Procrastination is one of the biggest stumbling blocks that trip up students on the road to academic success and higher grades. The temptation to procrastinate is part of human nature, and procrastination is especially tempting when the task at hand is unpleasant.

Moreover, a dreadful assignment does not go away if you put it off. Rather, it festers like an infected wound until the only solution is amputation. That is: if you procrastinate long enough, you will sacrifice something valuable. In this case, your sacrifice will be your final grade. Procrastination is a ticket to academic failure.

Instead of procrastinating, create a priority list every day before you start doing homework. Arrange your list based on the impact each assignment will have on your final grade. Remember that even though you may enjoy making that cute collage of the 1960s or coloring the pretty DNA diagram for science, right now it may be much more important to study your notes for the algebra test. "But it's *boring*—so tedious!" you say. So what? Just be bored. It won't kill you. Do you want higher grades? If you do, the price you often must pay is doing the tough or boring assignments first and the fun ones last.

ACTION PLAN

1. Keep a work planner and prioritize your assignments by their impact on your final grade for the class.

2. Write next to each assignment the amount of time you estimate it will take, so that you can plan each evening accordingly.

3. If you have a big assignment or a big test, plan to do a little of the work each day. Don't lie to yourself that it is better to do all the work right before the assignment is due or the test is given, so that you won't forget the material. That is just an excuse. That strategy doesn't work.

4. Remember that study is not productive if you do it when you should be sleeping, and that studying smart may have a great impact on your final grade. (Review Chapter 21 for a refresher course on effective studying.)

5. Make a vow not to procrastinate—no matter what—for one six-week stretch. Most habits are formed within six weeks, so if you can avoid procrastinating for that long, you will have broken your bad old habit and built a good new one. You probably won't have a problem with procrastination again.

6. Don't procrastinate with the last suggestion. Do it right now.

7. Think about the following questions and discuss them with your classmates:

- Do you procrastinate? Why or why not?

- Give an example, if you have one, of how procrastinating has turned out badly for you.

- How important is it to academic success to avoid procrastination?

- What lessons can you take away from this chapter?

CHAPTER 27
Making Standardized Tests Matter

At one high school, two to four weeks before the big state standardized test, teachers begin giving released practice questions as classwork, homework, or extra credit. Students practice away. Many teachers go over test-taking strategies and give great speeches as to why this test matters. They tell students how important their test results are to the school's reputation. Some instructors even fib about the consequences to motivate students. But in the end, little of this effort proves productive.

When the test results come back, they are disappointing. The principal notices that about 250 students used their answer sheets to bubble in gang symbols, profanity, and other creative remarks. The principal pulls these students aside before the next state test and begs them to take the test seriously. As an incentive, he offers a pizza party. Yes, there are better incentives, as we will soon discuss, but what happens? The school meets its Adequate Yearly Progress (AYP) and Academic Performance Index (API) goals. Having an incentive other than the school's reputation makes the difference. This method seems to accomplish far more than all the practice questions and test-taking strategies. Most importantly, students are making academic progress despite themselves.

What can we learn from this example? The right motivation matters. What motivates students to study for and give their best on a state test? What motivates students to listen to lectures and follow the lesson objectives all year? It isn't their school's reputation, that's for sure. It's got to be something that benefits students personally. A pizza party is one motivator. But here's an even better one: making the standardized test count toward the final grade in class.

Reasons for Integrating Standardized Tests with Grading

Many students will work hard for a good grade. (If you have students who don't think grades are important, review Chapter 17 with your class.) The final grade may be the best tool for changing student behavior that most teachers know how to use effectively.

Let's look at this logically. If a standardized test is valid, and if it measures what it claims to measure, then it should already connect to what's being taught in the classroom. Teachers are supposed to be helping students learn according to state standards. And state standardized tests are supposed to measure students' progress toward learning that material. Therefore, these tests can be an appropriate component of the final grade. When students are convinced that the test matters to them personally and that it is relevant to the work they do all year long, overall they will score higher. This strategy is a much better motivator than knowing that the test will help the school's reputation. It might even be a better motivator than pizza.

> What motivates students to study for and give their best on a state test? What motivates students to listen to lectures and follow the lesson objectives all year? It isn't their school's reputation, that's for sure. It's got to be something that benefits students personally. A pizza party is one motivator. But here's an even better one: making the standardized test count toward the final grade in class.

But how can a standardized state test connect to the final grade when in most cases, the results come back after teachers submit the final grades? The answer is simple: change student transcripts if necessary to reward students for their achievement. You will need administration approval. Likely you will get it. Administrators, too, want accountability attached to standardized tests—perhaps even more than teachers do, because much of their job security immediately depends upon it. My principal was eager to cooperate with this plan. If your administrators are hesitant, then give them this chapter to read. Ask them to consider the benefits of this approach:

- Students see that they can fix past mistakes affecting their classroom grade by scoring well on state tests. This is important, because some students give up after making mistakes in the early weeks of school—and they stay checked out for the rest of the year. Linking state tests with final grades gives these students a reason to keep working. All year long, you can remind students not to quit, because everything they are learning can make a difference in the end.

- When more students stay checked in all year, a more positive classroom environment results. Just a few hopeless, checked-out students in a class can cause major disruptions and affect everyone's academic performance.

- You can apply the same principle of erasing past mistakes to unit or benchmark tests throughout the year, continually bringing students back into the education process with a series of second chances.

How to Integrate Standardized Testing with Grading

How do you actually use a standardized test in your final grading calculations? Try one of these five approaches. (Remember that you never need to lower a student's grade because of low standardized test performance. Our goal here is to motivate, not to create unnecessary test anxiety.)

Grade-Bump Approach I

Make the standardized test worth a 10 percent grade bump of the final grade for your class. Or use whatever percentage you believe is fair and logical—as long as the test is worth something. For example, let's say you want all the work in your class to be worth 1,000 points. And you want the state test to be worth a 10 percent grade bump of the final grade. Make the general assignments, participation, and tests worth 1,000 points and the state test worth 100 points. If a student scores 70 percent on the state test, enter that score as 70 extra credit points. If you don't get the state test results back in time, then you must be willing to change student transcripts.

Grade-Bump Approach II

Let's use the California Standards Test as an example. The CST classifies scores in five tiers: far below basic, below basic, basic, proficient, and advanced. If a student currently has a score of 67 percent in your class but scores in the proficient tier on the CST, give perhaps a 3 to 6 percent grade bump. If the student scores in the advanced tier on the CST, give perhaps a 7 to 10 percent grade bump in your final tally. The point here is not the exact percentage of the grade bump but the fact that an incentive is agreed upon before the state test.

The Extra-Credit Approach

With this approach, you treat the standardized test as extra credit. Let's use the CST as an example again. Here are some possibilities:

- Give students 1 extra-credit point for each state test question they answer correctly.

- Give students 100 extra-credit points for moving up a tier from last year.

- Give students 10 extra-credit points for each percentage point they improve over last year's state test score.

Of course, it is more difficult for a student who is already in the highest tier to benefit from a higher score. In this case, you could offer points for staying in the top tiers or for not dropping a tier.

The Other-Rewards Approach

If you feel strongly that standardized tests should not figure in to your students' final grades, you could motivate them to do well on the state test in a different way. Consider other rewards not directly connected to the final grade, such as:

- A certificate of recognition

- A homework pass

- Listing on a wall of fame in your classroom

- A pizza party

The Combination Approach

Use the parts of these suggestions that fit your philosophy. Use them to brainstorm other ideas.

ACTION PLAN

1. Motivate students to take standardized test seriously by connecting the results to their final grade. There are several ways to do this.

2. Consider each of the various methods for connecting test scores with grades by discussing the following questions with your school's administrators and your fellow teachers:

   • What ideas do you like in this approach?

   • What problems do you see with this approach?

   • How could this approach be modified to fit our needs?

   • What action plan should we implement?

3. More than grades motivate students. Try a wall of fame with categories such as "most improved," "highest score," "proficient," and "advanced."

4. Each quarter give a practice test. Give one extra-credit point for each question answered correctly. This will help ensure that students give their best effort. Training and practice will improve test scores.

5. Hold a Socratic Seminar with your students using the reproducible handout "Why This Test Should Matter to You Personally" on page 171.

Socratic Seminar: Why This Test Should Matter to You Personally

Questions for Discussion

1. If I put $1 million in cash on your desk and said you could keep it if you score proficient or higher on the state test, would you score higher this year?

2. What is the incentive teachers and administrators offer for taking the state test?

3. What should the incentive be? What would motivate you?

4. Why are state tests so important to teachers and administrators?

5. How do you feel about taking these tests?

6. What can teachers and administrators do to help you do your best on the state test?

7. What can your parents or other family members do to help you?

8. What is the general attitude among students in this school about state testing?

9. How could this attitude be improved?

PART 2 SUMMARY

Why should you help students understand such things as teacher nuances, the weighted grade, extra credit, avoiding zeros, turning in late work, the devastation of procrastination, and the importance of standardized tests, to name just a few of the topics covered in this section of the book? I mean, really: is it your job to teach this material? You are a history (math, science, English, insert subject here) teacher. You barely have time to cover the standards, and yet I am suggesting all this extra curriculum. Have I lost my mind?

No, not at all. These topics are not an additional curriculum. Rather, they are absolutely essential information if students are to learn your subject matter and succeed in your class. The information in Part 2 of this book is a primer on navigating our educational system. We must teach the framework by which students are judged if we expect them to succeed within that framework. We cannot ignore the reality that many students fail not because they haven't mastered the standards but because they haven't mastered the system. One missing assignment can drop a student's grade from an A to a D even though that one assignment gives little true evaluation of the student's abilities in your subject area.

> We must teach the framework by which students are judged if we expect them to succeed within that framework. We cannot ignore the reality that many students fail not because they haven't mastered the standards but because they haven't mastered the system.

The grading system found in most U.S. schools is a great mystery to many students. Many middle school and high school students have no idea how and why they get the grades they get. Such mysteries breed anger, discontent, and failure. And it is not their fault—at least not completely.

We educators must teach our students how to master the U.S. educational system—flawed though it is. Read Part 2 with them in class and discuss the points made in each chapter. From start to finish, this process may take one or two weeks of class time, but it will pay you back with a whole semester of higher-quality work and better attitudes. In the long run, this investment will save you and your students much time. Time once wasted on logistics can now be spent on content and skills. If you think, "This is not my job," or, "I don't have time to teach this," I believe you are mistaken. Spending a week or two explaining the system makes far more sense than spending a semester battling ignorance of the system and the mistakes that creates. This is the way to open up more time for teaching the standards.

PART 2 ACTION PLAN
Teach Your Students the Path to Higher Grades

You might want to attach this list to the front cover of your lesson planning book.

1. **Foster more reading!** If your students don't like to read, and you have too much on your plate to correct reading assignments every day, use the sworn statement method outlined in Chapter 14. It addresses both problems effectively.

2. **Please, teach your students how to be organized.** You may be their last hope in mastering this important skill. It will bring you great satisfaction and reduce your workload. Chapter 15 can help you.

3. **Your students got attitude?** The Socratic Seminar is just one of the attitude adjustment techniques discussed in Chapter 16. Try this direct approach to changing attitudes. It works.

4. **Teaching individual responsibility pays dividends.** Take the time to help students resist grade-related peer pressure using the strategies described in Chapter 17. Don't glorify the D culture.

5. **Don't let students pigeonhole themselves.** Student success in your class improves dramatically when you help students see that they are not destined to be A, B, C, D, or F students. Chapter 18 argues that it is worth the effort to show students the path to academic success.

6. **Teach the math behind the grades.** Academic failure is often due to unawareness of the nuances found in teacher grading systems. Students need your help navigating the logistics of a grade. Chapter 19 can help you help your students.

7. **Don't allow your students to play the shy card.** Show them how to participate in your class. The real world requires that they speak up. Guide them along this path using the ideas in Chapter 20.

$\longrightarrow$

8. **Students often have no idea how and what to study.** Use Chapter 21 to help direct your students toward meeting your learning objectives. Teach them how to study effectively for tests.

9. **Offer extra credit.** Not all teachers use extra credit, but many do. With the ideas in Chapter 22, you can help your students see the impact extra-credit work can have on their final grade.

10. **Show students the impact of a zero grade.** Perhaps the greatest grade destroyer of them all is the missing assignment. Help students avoid this unnecessary fate. Chapter 23 shows what a zero does to grade percentages. It will motivate your students more than a great speech.

11. **How do you feel about late work?** Chapter 24 addresses this common problem. Read this chapter to your students. It will encourage your students to work harder for you and turn in their work on time.

12. **What if all your students could become just a little bit more likable?** Your job satisfaction and their performance would both improve. Read Chapter 25 to your students. This is a lesson many of them need.

13. **Don't procrastinate on reviewing Chapter 26.** Train your students to tackle their most important work head-on. Breaking the student habit of procrastination is not as hard as you might think.

14. **Do your students simply not care about standardized tests?** Then you need to motivate them with incentives that matter to students personally. Chapter 27 will show you how.

APPENDIX

Worksheets to Help Your Students Improve Their Grades

Read the following worksheet descriptions and find the ones that apply to specific students in your class. Give the appropriate worksheets to the students who need them, and encourage them to put the worksheets in their notebooks.

Worksheet 1: for the student who works hard but does poorly on tests

Worksheet 2: for the student who does not do the work but does well on tests

Worksheet 3: for the student who does not turn in work and does poorly on tests but listens and behaves well in class

Worksheet 4: for the student who behaves poorly but is actually quite bright

Worksheet 5: for the student who is disorganized

Worksheet 6: for the student with low expectations

Worksheet 7: for the student who is stressed out by perfectionism

Worksheet 8: for the student who is easily bored or has a tiny attention span

Worksheet 9: for the student who is focused more on friends than academics

Worksheet 10: for the student who is in an academic hole because of low attendance or past mistakes

Cracking the Teacher-Created Test

On this type of test, questions are created by the teacher, not the publishers of the textbook or an online test bank.

Analyze the test and circle all the following descriptors that apply:

a. Vocabulary-driven
b. Lecture-driven
c. Homework- and classwork-driven
d. Textbook-driven
e. Mystery-driven

The formula:

a. If the test is vocabulary-driven, make flash cards and study them. Have a friend test you; it's more fun that way.

b. If the test is lecture-driven, take notes during lectures and study the notes.

c. If the test is homework- and classwork-driven, complete the work and keep it to study later.

d. If the test is textbook-driven, go online to the publisher's website. Go to the teacher section and preview the questions.

e. If the test is mystery-driven, ask your teacher how she or he creates tests and what you should study. Apply strategies A through D above, depending on the answer you get.

Cracking the Outside-Source Test

Ask your teacher about the source of the test.

Circle all that apply:

a. Test bank of questions from textbook publishers
b. Test bank from another source online
c. Test bank hard copy from publishers
d. Teacher won't say
e. Some questions from the publishers and some teacher-created

The formula:

a. Go online and preview the test.
b. Go online and preview the test.
c. Visit the publisher's website. In most cases, the teacher's hard copy and the online version are similar.
d. Examine your first returned test. You should be able to tell how it was created.
e. Follow the steps above, mixing and matching as needed.

Keep this handout in your notebook and remind yourself of the following points.

Why Do Homework If I Do Well on Tests?

1 **Why do work outside of class?** Because it is in my best interest. There is no reason to drop my grade even as little as 10 percent in order to avoid a few minutes of work each day.

2 **I have no time—when am I supposed to do homework?** Complete the work during class downtime. Every class has a few moments of wasted time during the course of the day. I could also complete the work on my commute to school or schedule some time after dinner or during the first hour after school.

3 **Why does it matter so much?** Homework is not going away as long as I am in school. Completing my assignments with a positive attitude means less stress and energy for me in the long run. Parents and teachers will be easier to deal with in the future. I owe it to myself to build my reputation instead of tearing it down.

4 **How can I get in the habit of doing my homework?** I can set a goal to work just five more minutes each day on each class, then increase that goal by five minutes each month. I might find that dedicating less than thirty minutes per day can permanently improve my habits.

5 **Here is my plan:**

_____

_____

_____

_____

_____

Worksheet 3

Keep this handout in your notebook and remind yourself of the following points.

Problem One: You Don't Do Homework

1 It is time to change. Get an assignment notebook—one that is simple and easy to use. Record your assignments and check them off as you complete them. This is easy and quick, and it works.

2 Ask a friend who does not have your problem to hold you accountable. Agree on the consequences if you fail to complete your work. A plan without consequences is not a plan. Make the consequence serious but not ridiculous, such as no playing video games, no texting, and no computer until you finish all your work.

3 Agree with your friend on a reward for academic success, such as going to a theme park, movie, or concert together—a theme park for semester improvements, a concert for quarter improvements, and a movie for homework completed two weeks in a row or significant test improvement.

Problem Two: You Have Poor Test Scores

1 Use Worksheet 1.

2 Take a returned test and show it to a friend who is a good test taker. Ask your friend the following questions, and encourage blunt answers: "What do I need to do to score higher? What would you do if this happened to you?" Expect sarcasm from your friend. After you laugh a bit, you will get good advice. People love to be looked up to as experts.

3 Talk to your teacher. This is a good idea, because your calm and responsible behavior will speak volumes. Teachers are looking for ways to reward students like you. Don't miss out on the possibilities of academic success because you are shy or embarrassed. These feelings will pass.

4 Check your grades online daily. If you are going to stay motivated and kick your bad habits, then you need constant reminders of your progress. Keeping track of your grades will allow you to make adjustments before the work becomes too stressful and overwhelming.

Keep this handout in your notebook and remind yourself of the following points.

The Ten Pillars of School Behavior

1. I don't need to like this teacher to do the work for this class.

2. I don't need to challenge the teacher just because I am right.

3. Arguing with the teacher is not in my best interest—even if I am right.

4. Arguing with anyone in public hurts my reputation and grades.

5. My tone of voice matters. It could be wrongly interpreted and cause me problems.

6. Attitude is not invisible. I need to keep my body language in check.

7. I can cooperate now and voice my objections later.

8. Complaining will not help me in the long run.

9. Negative attention is worse for my grades than no attention at all.

10. Being likable is profitable for higher grades.

Graded Assignments: To-Do Checklist

Period one:

_____

_____

_____

All graded work for period one is completed and placed in my notebook or backpack or filed electronically so that I can turn it in on time. Initial here:

Period two:

_____

_____

_____

All graded work for period two is completed and placed in my notebook or backpack or filed electronically so that I can turn it in on time. Initial here:

Period three:

_____

_____

_____

All graded work for period three is completed and placed in my notebook or backpack or filed electronically so that I can turn it in on time. Initial here:

→

Period four:

_____

_____

_____

All graded work for period four is completed and placed in my notebook or backpack or filed electronically so that I can turn it in on time. Initial here:

Period five:

_____

_____

_____

All graded work for period five is completed and placed in my notebook or backpack or filed electronically so that I can turn it in on time. Initial here:

Period six:

_____

_____

_____

All graded work for period six is completed and placed in my notebook or backpack or filed electronically so that I can turn it in on time. Initial here:

Ten Truths to Boost Your Expectations

1 The difference mathematically between an A or a B can be one point on one assignment over the course of a semester.

2 One extra comment during a class discussion could provide that extra participation point.

3 Spending one second more on a multiple-choice test could help you see the obvious answer.

4 One extra sentence on an essay could give one point more.

5 One more answer on a worksheet could give you an A instead of a B.

6 One more question after class or one more smile upon entering the room could give you the participation point you need.

7 One fewer grumble or one more offer to straighten the room after group work could give you an extra point. None of this has been preprogrammed.

8 You are in control. You can create good habits and change poor habits. Your academic habits play a large role in your determining grades. Listen, take notes, and read with a purpose. Be kind. Be humble. Show self-control.

9 Observe and imitate the work habits of A students as well as the textbook.

10 One point here and one point there make a difference over the course of a semester. Be organized. Keep track of your points.

Ten Commandments for the Highly Stressed

1 Keep an agenda book and prioritize your assignments.

2 Check off your assignments daily on a to-do list and then think about something else.

3 Write next to each assignment the amount of time you estimate it will take so that you can plan your evening.

4 Remember that study is not productive if you do it when you should be sleeping.

5 Even if your assignment is not perfect, turn it in anyway. Points are points, and points determine your final grade.

6 Reduce your grade anxiety or test anxiety by doing extra credit; it can make up for past mistakes and poor test scores.

7 Complete all opportunities for late work even if you will not get a perfect score on the work. Points are points, and points determine your final grade.

8 Don't spend large amounts of time on details that will not raise your grade. For example: That extra artwork on the history poster looks nice, but it does not raise your grade on the assignment. Don't do it.

9 Take some time to observe the students in your class who have good grades but are not obsessive. How do they do it?

10 Make a vow to yourself that when you stop working for the evening, you will not return to work or obsess about work. Change the channel on your mental TV set.

Worksheet 8

Keep the following list in your notebook to help you cultivate patience.

Ten Commandments for the Easily Bored

1. Remember that you have to sit in each class for almost an hour every day. When you look back at this period of your life, it might be nice to remember that you used this time for something useful.

2. Sit next to the students who seem to be the least bored. Ask them how they do it. Learn from their actions and words.

3. Avoid the friends who tempt you to veer off-track. Don't choose them for group work and don't sit next to them.

4. It may be more fun right now to zone out or talk about other things, but remember that making this behavior a habit will get you minimum wage for a lifetime.

5. Take notes no matter what. This will help you build your attention span. You need the ability to focus in order to succeed in life. Look at paying attention like exercising: it may not be fun, but the results are worthwhile.

6. Vow not to talk when the teacher is talking. Force yourself to repeat in your mind what the teacher is saying. If it is boring, then make it rhyme in your mind—or make it funny by changing it up a bit—but stay focused on the material.

7. Do not turn your head at every sound that happens in the classroom. Keep your eyes on the teacher or the task at hand.

8. Keep your body language in check. If you look bored and ready to pounce on a side conversation, then most likely one of your friends will see that and make it happen.

9. Force yourself to ask questions during lectures and instructions. As you formulate questions and listen to the answers, you will be building your attention span.

10. Give yourself an "attention span" grade in your agenda book every day so that you can look back and see your progress (or lack of progress) and adjust your efforts.

Ten Commandments for Social Butterflies

1. Are you addicted to texting? Set a limit and make a vow to keep it. Give yourself strong consequences.

2. Are you addicted to texting? Shut off your phone during class.

3. R U addicted 2 texting? Get tough with yourself. Do not text in the evening until after your homework is done—no matter what!

4. Add some friends to your circle who actually do schoolwork.

5. Sit next to the students who seem to be focused on the class, not on their friends. Ask them how they do it. Learn from their actions and words.

6. Set two or more hours after school for uninterrupted schoolwork—no peer contact at all.

7. Compare and contrast your social time and the time you spend doing academic work. Record the difference. Close the gap by putting more time toward schoolwork and less time toward socializing. You won't jeopardize your friendships, but you may just save your grades.

8. If you must spend time with friends after school, finish your schoolwork while you're at it. You will still have fun and spend time together.

9. Don't care too much about what other people think. Of what profit is this concern in the long run?

10. Remember that a real friend would want you to succeed in school.

Five Steps for Climbing Out of an Academic Hole

1. Get a printout of all your assignments. Study it.

2. Identify the cause of your poor grades and figure out how to explain it clearly to your teacher. Practice what you're going to say in your mind before you approach your teacher. Make sure that you place the responsibility completely on yourself. Be humble and likable. Remember, you want the teacher to take your side.

3. Discuss your situation with your teacher at an appropriate time. An appropriate time is when your teacher can give you full attention without the distraction of other duties, issues, and students (in other words, not between periods and not with a ton of other students around).

4. Negotiate points for late work and missing assignments, extra-credit opportunities, a chance to make up tests and zeros, and a chance to have assignments excused through extra work or forgiveness.

5. Keep your word and turn things in before or at the agreed time. Show a willing and grateful attitude.

RECOMMENDED RESOURCES

Breaux, Annette, and Todd Whitaker. *Seven Simple Secrets: What the Best Teachers Know and Do* (New York: Routledge, 2014). The "seven secrets" in this book are planning, classroom management, instruction, attitude, professionalism, effective discipline, and motivation. The book is full of tips and bulleted ideas on how to implement these secrets.

Clark, Ron. *The Excellent 11: Qualities Teachers and Parents Use to Motivate, Inspire, and Educate Children* (New York: Hyperion, 2004). The eleven qualities highlighted in this book include enthusiasm, adventure, compassion, balance, humor, common sense, creativity, and more. Using an anecdotal and narrative approach, Clark offers some practical suggestions on how to implement these qualities.

Dean, Ceri B., Elizabeth Ross Hubbell, Howard Pitler, and Bj Stone. *Classroom Instruction That Works: Research-Based Strategies for Increasing Student Achievement* (Alexandria, VA: ASCD, 2012). This book is more about how to teach than how to manage your workload and improve test scores. It is a good source for pedagogy.

Heyck-Merlin, Maia. *The Together Teacher: Plan Ahead, Get Organized, and Save Time!* (San Francisco: Jossey-Bass, 2012). Although this book is aimed mainly at elementary school teachers, it contains good advice on how to get organized.

Stronge, James H. *Qualities of Effective Teachers* (Alexandria, VA: ASCD, 2007). Stronge focuses on the preparation, personality, and practices of effective teachers. He focuses on teacher-controlled behaviors that contribute to student achievement, rather than factors that are outside a teacher's control.

Thompson, Julia G. *Discipline Survival Guide for the Secondary Teacher* (San Francisco: Jossey-Bass, 2011). Of course, this is a popular topic in education. Thompson's book offers 300 pages' worth of advice on accomplishing classroom discipline in secondary schools, using reader-friendly bulleted lists and step-by-step instructions.

www.avid.org
Advancement Via Individual Determination (AVID) trains educators to use proven practices to prepare students for success in high school and college. Explore the organization's website to learn about the program and its methodologies. Some states have their own AVID offices; see the "contact" section of the website for addresses and phone numbers of these and the central headquarters.

INDEX

Patrick Kelley, M.A., has a master's degree in curriculum and instruction from California State University San Bernardino and a bachelor's degree in history from Castleton State College in Vermont. He has been a classroom teacher for more than twenty-five years. He has experience as a mentor teacher and an AP coordinator as well as ten years of experience with the AVID program. He is certified in Gifted and Talented Education (GATE) and currently works with the International Baccalaureate program. Patrick provides workshops and presentations to districts, schools, and teams. To contact him, visit www.patrickkelleybooks.com.

More Great Books from Free Spirit

When Gifted Kids Don't Have All the Answers
How to Meet Their Social and Emotional Needs (Revised and Updated Edition)
by Judy Galbraith, M.A., and Jim Delisle, Ph.D.
288 pp., PB, 7¼" x 9¼".
Teachers, gifted coordinators, guidance counselors, and parents of gifted children.
Includes digital content.

The Common Sense Guide to the Common Core
Teacher-Tested Tools for Implementation
by Katherine McKnight, Ph.D.
240 pp., PB, 8½" x 11".
K–12 teachers, administrators, district leaders, curriculum directors, coaches, PLCs, preservice teachers, university professors.
Includes digital content.

The Gifted Teen Survival Guide
Smart, Sharp, and Ready for (Almost) Anything
by Judy Galbraith, M.A., and Jim Delisle, Ph.D.
272 pp., PB, 7" x 9".
Ages 11 & up.

The Principal's Survival Guide
Where Do I Start? How Do I Succeed? When Do I Sleep?
by Susan Stone Kessler, Ed.D., April M. Snodgrass, M.Ed., and Andrew T. Davis, Ed.D.
208 pp., PB, 7¼" x 9¼".
Principals and administrators K–12.

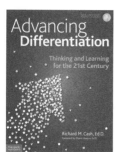

Advancing Differentiation
Thinking and Learning for the 21st Century
by Richard M. Cash, Ed.D.
224 pp., PB, 8½" x 11".
K–12 teachers and administrators.
Includes digital content.

Building Everyday Leadership in All Teens
Promoting Attitudes and Actions for Respect and Success (Curriculum Guide for Teachers and Youthworkers)
by Mariam G. MacGregor, M.S.
240 pp., PB, 8½" x 11".
Teachers and youthworkers grades 6–12.